How To Slack Your Way To Success

By Tommy v2 and Zor

Dedicated to our fans: past, present, future… even the annoying ones. ~~That means you, Bhupi.~~

The following book contains depictions of true events. The names of all third-parties have been mildly modified for their own protection. This protection may include matters of legal implication, embarrassment or downright shaming them because they did something totally inappropriate and/or stupid. It is of no fault of these third-parties that we are smarter and cleverer, back then and to this day.

Reader discretion is advised.

The Formula for Success

As we've been saying (and living) for years, everything you do and have done distills down to one single concept:

Degree of success = results ÷ effort

That's it.

Let me explain it in even simpler terms in case some part of your brain either doesn't understand or - heaven forbid - disagrees.

Fact: Johnny and Tammy are of identical intelligence and ability.

A) Johnny gets an 8/10 on his test after studying all night and working his ass off.

B) Tammy gets a 7/10 on her test after playing Street Fighter II Turbo all night long and never opening the text book once. She is simply going off what she remembered from class.

As you can clearly see, Tammy comes out the winner here. Simply, her degree of success, based on our formula, is clearly higher.

Now, let's extrapolate this to a higher level.

A) Johnny continues to work hard at all his subjects. Unfortunately, there is simply not enough time to handle them all, so by focusing on one, his other subjects suffer. He gets 8/10 on one test, but bombs and gets 5/10 on another. 6/10 on yet another. The harder he studies, the more the other subjects suffer. He becomes a mediocre student, suffers from constant high levels of stress and anxiety which cause him to downward spiral into the Saturday night shift at Burger King until he's 37, oftentimes seeing paystubs so low that he studies the location of the decimal point *very* carefully.

B) Tammy, now well-rested and *still* trying to understand the appeal of Dr. Mario after playing it all afternoon, continues to churn out 7/10 tests continuously. Could she study and do better? Sure. Of course, that would break the efficiency of her method. She continues to enjoy her life and free time, being a solid B student. She now works for Burger King's head office in the HR department earning an honest $42,000/year with full benefits. She even attended the corporate Christmas party with no ill-will or ethical reservations and even treated her co-worker Alex to a vodka cranberry.

It becomes obvious now, doesn't it? The human body and brain is only capable of so much energy output. You have to decide how you're going to spend it. Some people focus and become great writers, but maybe they have no time to cut the grass and piss off their wives. Others are terrific athletes but you wouldn't trust them with index fund investment ideas. Others yet, like *us*, make a point of not wasting any energy on the useless stuff in life. We simply plug in our formula to decide if it's worth it. Do I spend 2 hours to write a 7/10 essay or do I spend an entire weekend doing it, then handing it off to 3 people for opinions and edits, just to get that 8.5/10? What is that 1.5 worth? The answer is that it's not worth shit. Its intrinsic value nears zero the longer you work at it.

That's how you slack your way to success. We have and will continue to implement our formula in all aspects of our lives, from breakfast alone at the train station to all-nighter gaming sessions with our best friends. This is our life story and we've worked hard to share it with you. All you have to do is *read* it - it looks like you're already part of the formula.

-v2 and Zor

The Earliest Years

v2's Account

In writing a book, I have this amazing invention called a *time machine*. It's a literary device that moves things into the future so you don't get bored with my crappy origin story. Here's an example of how I can get through the first 6 years of MY LIFE in a single paragraph at breakneck speed.

Born in Poland in 1982. Survived Chernobyl in 1986. Came to Canada in 1987 without obvious nuclear mutations. Tried McDonald's. Went to elementary school where they played with blocks as part of the curriculum. Met Zor in class. TIME MACHINE MAXIMUM SPEED >>>> I'm writing about it today using a web browser with a sans-serif font.

And to think, some people write an entire book about their childhoods when I did that shit with disgusting efficiency.

Let's back up to the start of Grade 1 when I met Zor. That's really my first social interaction, since going to school in Poland was little more than constant being hit on the head with a wooden ruler by nuns because you made an error during your long-division problem AT AGE FIVE. Yes, actually. We had to compete with the Chinese somehow, as if we predicted their domination 20 years later.

So of all the kids that were willing/tolerant of hanging out with some pretty blonde immigrant kid (I really *was* a beautiful boy until I wasn't), I was most interested in hanging out with this kid named James. Something about that kid just worked for me and I was desperate to make friends in this strange and wonderful country / city / school / playground. Like all social beings, James was not exclusive. He had *other* friends. Friends other than *me*. It was an upsetting little tidbit, and it didn't sit well with me at all. Time was limited, at recess he could hang out with other dudes. Since I'm a possessive control freak with a low self-esteem, this was unacceptable. As time went on, he started spending a lot of time with this kid Zor, some goofy little bastard that came from some rich-ass house (or so I heard). Already at this age, the psychological warfare had begun.

"James... if you keep hanging out with that guy, I won't be your friend anymore," I proclaimed, entirely sure that this was the correct move.

"Well, whatever," he replied in his finest 1989 childhood voice. "*I don't give a care.*"

This sob story continued for months with Zor and I competing for James' time and attention. Bribery. Favours. Blackmail. I heard that one time, Zor even gave him his little cheese and crackers kit (the one with the red stick). I couldn't compete with that. I was stickless and cracker-free, being a poor immigrant that had to eat healthy food to survive.

...then, one fateful day, the word on the street was out: *James was moving away.* At that age, it's worse than death. It's worse than watching your older brother flush your gerbil down the toilet while the thing squeals and squirms around by the strength of its meaty tail. If nothing else, Zor and I mourned the loss of our mutual friend James together. We swapped stories and compared notes, always employing the fine art of one-upsmanship at every given opportunity.

...and then it happened: Zor and I became friends better than James and I ever could. He was a better, smarter, more interesting person. If that wasn't enough, two more earth-shattering factors were revealed that changed the very fabric of our space and time: Zor had a Nintendo Entertainment System and he was within *walking distance of my house.*

Zor's Account

I was the child of an immigrant family. The whole "we came to the country with nothing but five dollars in my pocket and then found middle-class success" described my family exactly. My parents would never let me forget it. Forget getting smacked in the head by nuns at school, my parents would whip my ass if I ever got out of line. The rules of the house were simple: don't waste money, don't step out of line and pay attention in school.

As for the whole ordeal with James, the school we both attended housed many children of immigrant families (read: low income neighborhood). We were all goofy bastards and I never had problems making friends in school; James being no exception. We hung out and all I remember about v2 was the blonde kid who tried way too hard to be accepted by his peers. However, I do remember him being much smarter than everyone else and being able to read above his grade level.

One day James moved away. This is a devastating blow because all the rest of the class talked about was sports and construction, which bored the shit out of me. I, on the other hand, learned how to read at the age of three because books were awesome and Lavar Burton kept telling me not to take *his* word for it. Reading also makes you a more interesting person who can go beyond shallow bullshit. QFT.

The only interesting person left in the class to hang out

with was v2. I found out he not only knew what a Nintendo was, he could also tell me about the intricacies of its games, despite him never owning one.

Eventually, he would introduce me to the richness of the world including Chip & Dale Rescue Rangers, Sega Genesis, Jaws and how much better v2 was at writing.

While I could read like nobody's business, my writing was always too confusing - too many thoughts trying to be crammed into one sentence. This bad habit would plague me all the way until University when I cut that shit out. However, my jealousy for the elegant, straightforward prose of v2 in our little budget journals always drove me nuts. I may have been an A-student, but v2 was an A-writer. In time my jealousy would subside and it all started with a birthday trip to Toys 'R Us...

v2:

My 9th birthday back in February 1991 was bittersweet. Mostly sweet, but some real fucking nasty parts.

It was the only birthday besides my 18th, 19th and 31st that people actually gave a shit about. My parents threw me a party and I invited a few classmates and friends. Also worth mentioning that I invited this girl named Michelle, who was my first love and conveniently lived across the hall from me in our apartment building. People abuse the word "literally" all the time, so I have to emphasize that when you opened our apartment door of 202, 201 was ACTUALLY across the hall. There's where Michelle lived. At any given point, I was no more than 10 meters away from her and it was sort of romantic now that I think about it. Back then I just thought that she was going to be my wife so there was no value in getting all bent out of shape over it.

Before the party began, my dad and I picked up Zor to make a run to Toys 'R Us, where I was allowed to pick any Sega Genesis game I wanted. I seriously eyeballed Thunder Force II and Strider, but somehow my stupid child mind thought that buying *Columns*, a puzzle game, was the right move. I told myself dumb shit like "puzzle games have infinite replay value" and "a game is better when it never ends." My dad paid the painful $59.99 plus tax and we brought home the game just in time for the party.

The party itself was a blast, with all of my company bringing me amazing gifts, especially Zor who bought me a Ninja Turtles action figure. Well, his parents certainly did, but that's beside the point. The party was all shenanigans and good times but there was one particular guest that required a different kind of attention. His name was Mike, and right from the get-go we knew that he'd be on a trashy talk show one day about his white-trash accomplishments.

Zor:

Mike's condition can only be described as "what the *hell*, guy?" He kept bouncing off the walls and wouldn't shut his mouth for longer than half a second. When two other nine-year-old boys think he's acting ridiculous and want him to stop, you know something isn't right. Here we are, v2's 9th birthday party, trying to enjoy some Columns and having it ruined by Mike who felt the game lacked action. This was followed by v2 attempting to tell a hilarious story (he was a storyteller for as long as I remember) and this kid just wouldn't shut up and kept bouncing across the room.

I'm not a violent man. I have fantasies of things I would do to people if I became dictator of the world, but it always comes from a sense of justice. I've never considered violence a first resort and while I had a short temper as a kid, my way of blowing off steam was to disappear until I calmed down. However, Mike had pushed me past my threshold of patience. After watching him jump up and down on v2's bed, thereby ruining the fun we were having, I took action.

In one motion, I grabbed a boomerang v2 had in his bedroom (yes, a fucking boomerang) and full-force swung it at Mike's ass. No sound effect would do justice to the scene. The guy went down in a heap and I stood over top of him yelling to shut his mouth. The whimpers that came from his mouth were followed by deep panting as he made no effort to move again for the entire night.

That's really where the formula all started.

Had we done this at the *beginning* of the night, we would've had a kick-ass time. We spent all our energy in patience and pleading when a swift beating with a boomerang is all it took. Unfortunately, v2 and I didn't learn our lesson that day and another incident came up with our friend Mike. Let me sum-up that ordeal: Mike stole $60 from v2's place, denied it and finally admitted it to his parents the next day. He then stole baseball cards from me a week later. We stopped hanging out with the guy.

As for our prediction on where he would end up in life - a few years ago he was on the Maury show. And yes, he was the father.

The forced meeting as a result of James and ordeal with Mike led v2 and I to understand we had a different kind of friendship. It was based around intelligence, ambition, achieving great goals and doing it all together. We played video games (something not common during the time), read books and understood how to manipulate the entire school yard.

It took no effort for our friendship to thrive. Neither of us had to really try because we both understood our creativity complimented each other. Our friendship was the earliest form of our formula and at the time, we couldn't achieve a higher form of success. We lived across the street from each other, hung out all the time and always had great memories. At the age of 9, we learned what success meant.

Then, v2's parents hit the big time and he moved away. His new house was an entire five minute drive from my place, but when you're a kid, a five minute drive anywhere is astronomically far. We slowly lost contact, but you can't keep a good thing down.

Especially when you re-unite in high school.

The High School Years

The Only Lesson You Need

Zor:

High School makes for some interesting years in your life. From an education standpoint, cramming a bunch of teenagers who don't give a shit into one room and trying to force algebra down their throats, no matter how hard you try to differentiate instruction, is asking for an aneurysm. Those who *are* motivated to succeed will do so without any prodding from their teachers, sometimes in spite of them. Those who aren't motivated will wash away in the drudgery of their lives until the day they pull themselves back together.

Plugging our formula into the high school years, we can see how easy it is to be on the losing end. However, if there's one thing we learned about high school it's this:

High school doesn't dictate the kind of person you're going to be for the rest of your life.

Having met people who barely passed high school only to move on and become lawyers, rockstars and millionaires, it makes no sense to put the pressure on to overachieve. Some of the overachievers we went to high school with went on to study engineering and medicine, only to quit years later and teach rock climbing in California. Hell, I didn't even finish with the proper credits to get into University and I still managed to get two degrees, a Masters and an offer to teach Undergraduate courses. That's not to say v2 and I were dicks to our teachers - quite the opposite. We just learned how to enjoy the time and achieve the highest levels of success you can get with high school: graduate on time and GTFO.

Slacking Off in Communications Class

Communications class is the single greatest high school course you could've taken circa 1996-2000. The entire course was self-guided. The first year you take the class, you are given a list of projects to complete in a timeframe. One of them was to make a business card in a *week*. That should give you an indication of the course's difficulty.

The later years were projects that *you* created and set the due dates for their completion. If you're a half-conscious, half-decent human being, the only reason you didn't get 100% in the course is because you weren't motivated enough to look at the checklist of what was required for each assignment.

Our high school also piloted a test program that trained high school students to pass industry certification exams: A+, Network+ and eventually CCNA. We spent our last year of high school taking nothing but communications credits.

Here's what we learned:

- Buying a video game system just to play one video game isn't a ridiculous idea.

- The most brutal thing you could do to someone is powerbomb them through a lectern, as we fantasized about doing to some people

- While screwing around on the computer during class, I blurt out the line (in reference to a video game, of course), "it's smaller for more accuracy." To this day, truer words have never been spoken.

- Kids with A+ Certifications did NOT earn $30/hr being computer techs, which is the dream they sold us for taking the pilot course

- Comptia earned a lot of money from high school students taking industry exams
- It's *not* the best class for oogling hot women
- We had limits and standards for getting laid

What!? Limits? Standards? What do you mean?

When you're awesome like us, women want to be with you. Little did we know, but we both got the interest of the same girl who made us go through the same situation. In fact, it doesn't matter who tells this story because the exact same thing happened to both of us. There is only a slight variation of the ending and it doesn't end well for any parties involved.

You want the story? We didn't sex her.

Anyway, thanks to Communications Classes, we passed high school with an excess amount of credits without putting in any effort. We spent most of our time yelling obscenities, bragging how hard we would bang the hottest girl in school and using school resources to win eBay auctions. Our teacher also won teacher of the year.

v2: The Importance of a Teacher, Even if the Subject is Stupid

I want to take some time to tell you about the most important teachers in my life, because I still think about them daily. Their importance in my life cannot be understated. This isn't nostalgia talking, either. This is TEH SRS BZNS.

Communications Class was by far the most important class I have ever attended. It was incredibly forward-thinking in its "do what you feel, bro" attitude and execution. Self-direction and internal motivation is easily the hardest thing to teach someone, let alone dumb teenagers like ourselves. The most important aspect of that class was the main teacher of the program. For privacy reasons, let's call him Mr. Clarke.

Mr. Clarke was the first teacher to see my true potential, but not in the "this kid is pretty smart" sort of way. He actively made sure I knew that kids like us were exactly his target audience. He even made a point of using our names when hyping up the future of our careers to the class. "Tom is now a fucking *millionaire*," he said, never. "All because he knew that Cisco routers were green and Juniper products were blue." It made the rest of the kids in class extremely jealous and make onlookers weep with blissful envy.

Mr. Clarke, being a smart man (smarter than most, for sure), also took it upon himself to supplement his income and ego by teaching other, advanced computer classes at a nearby college. He was double-ended-dildoing the educational system by making money off teaching the exact same thing twice every single day in two different places. Before we knew it, we were caught up in his far-fetched lies and promises of fat-stacking Benjamins just for knowing what the *deltree c:\windows*.** command did. It was a subtle version of the great speeches in *Boiler*

Room or *Glengarry Glen Ross* and we bought that shit wholesale. We spent our lunch breaks bragging about how we were going to drive our Porsches into bitches' houses just for fun because we were dot.com fuckers and would own the world.

Fast-forward to 2014 and the most amazing thing I've ever had happen to me is getting duplicate rebate cheque for a $39 video card. Mr. Clarke... *fuck you*. I did everything you ever said to do and I don't even have a gold toilet. But, to be fair, it's what made my career happen and it's been a successful one. I have a great day-job and it doesn't just pay the bills, *it actually makes bills for other people*. So there's that.

The second-most important teacher in my life is my Grade 9 and OAC (the former highest grade in Ontario) English teacher, let's call her Miss Kennedy... KENNEDY! Sorry, couldn't resist.

She was a bit of an odd duck as far as teachers went. She was brutally tough, handing out 80% grades for perfect work. However, she was friendly and personable. It didn't mesh in my head because most people who were tough were total Nazis. Because of my behavioral problems (which were numerous), I spent a lot of time with her in private talks as she tried to understand what my fucking major malfunction was. She just went with the cliché *bored genius* angle and treated me that way, always trying to bring out the best in me when I had nothing more to give than mediocrity and a poor attitude. Between scoldings about my shitty work ethic and apathy, she saw the potential. "You're the best writer in this class," she said, at least a dozen times. "But the best writing doesn't amount to anything in this class. You're not a good student."

There's nothing more to say about her. I made it my personal mission in life to succeed at being a famous writer who had the kind of groupies that she wished *she* had. Until the day I die, I won't stop trying to impress her, even if she doesn't even remember my existence. I don't care. My vendettas are forever. It was the beginning of our formula in practice as well - no matter how well we did, we only got an 80% in that class. So, naturally, I got a 61. I passed just as well as the brown-nosing over-achievers and I barely had to pay attention. I was too busy eating sunflower seeds and throwing the shells at the person sitting in front of me. On top of that, me, Zor and our old friend also took turns plagiarizing each other's book reports. Each week one of us would write it and the others would paraphrase it, earning lame but passable marks. The teacher caught onto our act but she couldn't prove shit, plus it was pretty competent. It was a great system for skipping the shitty work of actually reading the book and forming an opinion. *We* didn't need to, only the great hive mind needed to!

Next on the teacher docket is a tie, so I'm going to lump them in together. One is a science and physics teacher, and the other is a science and biology teacher.

Both of them taught me the same old lesson - just because I was a competent nerd didn't mean that I was destined for greatness. I would have to reach much higher in the years to come.

Lastly, and hardly least-importantly, the last teacher that did anything useful for me was a mean, short-tempered science and chemistry teacher, Mrs. Highkert.

She saw my potential but treated me like a common criminal. I was a problem child and that's how she handled me. She constantly kicked me out of glass for eating Doritos (like it's a crime, amirite?) and coming into class with headphones on. Guess she didn't like *The Crystal Method*? Years after high school had ended, I ran into her in the most unlikely of places - at a department store, selling perfume.

Shocked, I inquired further. She explained that she had enough of teaching and was pursuing her first love: dentistry. It was all cute and quaint until she uttered the most powerful words I had ever heard a teacher speak to me: "*It's because of students like you that I quit teaching.*"

It was a devastating statement and actually changed the fabric of my entire existence with a single lesson: *If you're an asshole, someone decent is going to hate you eventually.* I really didn't know what to do with my life after I had heard that. I guess I became a better person? Who knows? I still think about it. I go into that department store once a year or so, recalling the exact booth where my life was torn asunder. Well played, teach!

I hope you're a dentist now and I hope to one day make you realize that I'm a winner when I drive my Porsche right into the front of your house and fuck up your old tube TV where you watch game shows all night long.

Also, as an important side note, I found her incredibly hot. Tanned skin, limp, bleached-blonde hair, nice teeth (foreshadowing?) and a really bitchy face. She wore bitchy shoes, too - clearly uncomfortable but they were making a statement. The way she kept dealing with me as a total fuckup and yet handing me reasonable marks (I am a science kid, after all, and as long as math isn't involved I am pretty much legendary) really did wonders for my attraction to her. It might be a tad late now, but I should've looked her up years ago and got with her. I'd still be in my twenties then and if I showed up, I have no doubt that she'd be so intrigued that she'd... well... have heterosexual intercourse with me. I would assume she'd want to use the correct terminology and all that. We'd do something with covalent bonds and I'd isolate the variable or something. Who cares? With that hair, I'd let her call my mom to complain during the act if she wanted to.

Zor: You Don't Need to Learn Everything about Every Subject

We spend the early years of our education learning the basics. Our teachers are (hopefully) trained to provide us a foundation in a wide variety of subjects. If they did their job right, we get an inclination towards one of them. The next logical step would be to focus on that subject and become extremely good and masterful in the one area we love.

Instead, we have to continue the charade of learning everything about every subject for another four years. Becoming a "well-rounded" individual doesn't make you an extraordinary human being. It makes you another generic cog in a giant machine of mediocrity. Forget about being awesome at something - you can just be okay at a few things and really shitty at others. But don't worry; you'll forget everything the second you walk out the doors anyway.

If you're not motivated to like math and science by the time you reach high school, it's time to give up. Forcing the issue by continuing to take courses about something you'll never use again isn't going to help. It'll just make you hate high school even more. Unless, of course, your idea of science class is tearing off magnesium strips and setting them on fire; then by all means, burn, baby, burn!

In our Information Age, teachers aren't the gatekeepers to knowledge. If you want to go learn something, do the research yourself. Spending all your time trying to earn a high grade, which is superfluous and doesn't mean anything outside of school walls, is a wasted effort. Go learn what you need to for your mandatory credits and start focusing on something you enjoy.

Learning a little bit about every subject and failing to be

a master of something you like is a waste of time. All you become is an unfocused individual who kind of likes a few things but can't decide what you're really good at.

Then again, if you're trying to pick apart Shakespeare and still can't figure out the difference between *you're* and *your* – it's time to give up.

v2: Getting Away with Eating Taco Bell/Burger King/Pizza Hut Everyday

When you're young and your body is in superior functioning form, you can get away with a lot. Falls won't kill you, generally. You won't hurt your knees or back from lifting something heavier than you should. Most importantly, you can eat whatever the hell you want and it will barely make a dent on you.

Back in those days, we abused that policy to the extreme. At least 4 out of 5 weekdays we ate pizza, Taco Bell or Burger King. The odd time we'd go to the grocery store and each get a fucking pie to eat, followed by a 4-litre pail of ice cream and plastic spoons. It was reckless and strangely affordable, considering the amazing food we were eating.

My weakness was definitely Burger King. The incredible Whopper Junior was a mind-blowing 99 cents back then, which meant that eating *four* of them was a thing. Not just *any* old Whopper Junior, it was *heavy all, no onion* - the configuration of the gods. Mayo and lettuce jutted out of every crevice and distorted the intended geometry of this delicious concoction, rendering all other 99-cent items a laughable disappointment. I did this constantly and my physique never budged an inch, and neither did those of my friends. Success = result ÷ effort. Best food, easiest access and no downside. *Most successful lunch of all time.*

Zor: Keeping It Real

The two biggest mistakes you can make is taking high school too seriously and not putting enough effort to pass your classes. When you begin to think these magical things called 'marks' have an intrinsic connection to your self-worth, the real learning gets lost. When you fail a class because you couldn't put in enough effort to do the work, you're stuck taking the class over again. Both are a wasted effort.

Before HD cameras were the norm on cell phones... hell... before cell phones were even the norm, v2 saw the value in capturing everything important on film. We watch some of the footage now and can't help but admire how stupid we were when it came to life, but how clever we were when it came to creating memories.

In honor of Limp Bizkit, we wore different colored New York Yankees hats. People assumed we were in some sort of gang, especially when we all hung out together. It was our 'symbol of brotherhood.'

Before website design became point-and-click and Internet was fast enough to handle streaming video everywhere, we had video footage on a website we created about ourselves (I was a master of coding using Notepad).

We also exchanged services with a limo company - website design for free limo rides whenever we wanted. There's nothing more baller than pulling up to a concert with a limo and people wondering who the hell you are.

We purposely created our course schedule to have spares together, usually leading into, or following, lunch. If a class conflicted with hanging out with friends, we dropped it and found another time we could take it.

We acted like idiots, partied like nerds and ate like starving lions.

This isn't meant to be a treatise on the state of education. There are enough people out there shouting into the wind about that issue. What you did in high school and who you are as a person at the time, has little to no bearing on the rest of your life. High School should be a chance to explore, cause teenage drama and create memories that you still talk about fifteen years later.

That's how you exploit the formula during those years.

9 Months of Unaccredited College vs. Zor's Gillion Years in Academia

Zor:

Being a consummate slacker in high school was done for the sole purpose of our "post-secondary" plans. If you're wondering why I quoted post-secondary, it has everything to do with our college of choice. In order to satisfy our formula, we picked the best route for our skills and aptitude (which wasn't very high).

Thus, we selected a private college down the street

from us. It was one of those technical colleges that had ridiculously high tuition fees, no accreditation and used mainly to upgrade the skills of people currently in the industry. We both selected their "Network Engineering" Diploma, which would last one year and give us industry certifications from every company at the time.

Let's do a run-down of how "legit" this place was to attend:

- Classes ran for 4 hours in the morning. One of our instructors spent 3.5 of those hours playing video games on his laptop and 15 minutes skimming the chapters we were supposed to read in our books
- That same instructor also pulled his quiz/exam question from brain dumps online. Thanks to him, we all passed our industry exams because they were stolen from the Internet
- Their "job placement program" was a sassy woman (who we would totally both nail given the chance) who asked us what jobs we were interested in and whether we applied to them
- Microsoft Canada came to give a presentation to our school. Afterwards they offered a job to us to teach classes to upcoming high school students. v2 was smart enough to get cash from them upfront to buy burgers to think about the decision - the job never panned out
- I passed my UNIX exam while still drunk and barely

able to see the exam questions

- Recently, the college just teamed up with 2-4-1 Pizza to offer a $500 bursary to students

We spent every day doing fuck-all-of-nothing, got a bunch of industry certifications and got the hell out of there.

What happened?

v2 went off to find work and came up empty (see Call Centre chapter). After many runs of temp work, small contracts and bullshit employment, he finally landed a job where he does nothing but read NeoGAF all day while making mad bank and getting full benefits.

He bought a house with such a ridiculous down payment that his biggest worry is what he's going to do with endless amounts of disposable income.

I, on the other hand, took a year off before deciding I "really wanted to go to University." I spent four years doing my undergraduate degree, followed by a year of teacher's college (because I always "knew" I wanted to be a teacher), two years as a supply teacher and got a scholarship to go do my Masters.

After all that, I only managed to secure a few teaching contracts, got offered to teach an undergraduate class, which got cancelled, and spent many days figuring out the minimum amount I need to survive in today's world. The only thing that saved my ass was my side career as a professional magician. Something, by the way, you don't need to take business for in school to do (thankfully).

Am I bitter? Not really.

I actually enjoyed my time in university, but find it to be more of a self-fulfillment type of venue; something you do later in life when your brain naturally gravitates to that type of work.

Given our formula, v2 comes up the clear winner here. Since graduating, I've never worked harder in my life at gaining sustainable employment and the results haven't been thrilling. Most of the awesome things I do now are the result of my own side projects coming into fruition. Only time will tell whether our formula works itself out.

However, it does lead us to ways in which our formula is now being applied to the education system.

Taking Advantage of the Information Age

The Internet is a magical place. It can give you the entire collected knowledge of all of humanity and find it with simple searches.

To make things even easier, there are a few out there who have gone above and beyond the call of duty by releasing websites that will teach you in a structured manner. Here's a few that come to mind:

The Kahn Academy: everything you wanted to know about math... if you're into that kind of thing

Originally this started as some YouTube videos of a guy helping his family with their math homework. Millions of views later, it blew up into a full-on online academy.

There's a semi-linear progression for somebody to go from basic concepts to university level math work. This site fits our formula because you no longer want to slit your wrists every time you come across a math problem.

If you don't get it, you can go back and re-watch the lessons. There's also no self-esteem loss from getting the answer wrong. If you can't get a concept, you can keep trying until it sinks in.

With no pressure to pass exams, or figure out how to cheat off the guy beside you in class, you gain an astronomical amount of results from a decent amount of effort.

Coursera, Udacity and MITs FREE online courses

Take all the best professors from university, have them pick their best courses and put them online - free.

If you have any semblance of motivation, you can get an entire university education without paying for it. You won't get a fancy piece of paper to say you paid a gillion dollars for taking a bunch of courses, but the intrinsic value of the piece of paper falls below zero every year you live after getting it.

Wikipedia

How dare I suggest Wikipedia as a place to learn! It's not even a legitimate source in academic circles. You never know the type of information being put on there - it's not always accurate!

Do me a favour:

Go find an Encyclopedia Set from the 80s or 90s. Browse through some of the articles in there and tell me how accurate that information is and get back to me.

A digital database that can be updated as new information comes to light is the most powerful tool we have to gathering knowledge in one place.

All this being said, with a tiny bit of motivation and focus, there's no need for formal education. If you really need the structure, however, stick with one program to the end and leave it there. You will get the piece of paper stating you finished and anything you need to learn from this point on can be found elsewhere.

Unless you want to be something specialized like a doctor or pharmacist, don't go back to school for the sake of getting more education. The results diminish every time you do it.

Call Centers

Where Dreams Go to Die

How We Ended Up There
v2:

My experience with call centers used to be based on my limited experience asking for help when I was a child. The first phone call I ever made to anyone outside my friends and family was calling Nintendo Power for a subscription, simply putting my parents on for a minute to dole out the credit card information. My next call years later was Nintendo yet again, calling their Power Tip line so they could help me get past the water dungeon in Zelda: Link's Awakening.

These people were friendly, professional and they knew

their shit, even if they were reading from a text book.

Fast forward to many years later when we finally got Internet access. I called in to my ISP for several things (cable Internet in 1997 was a *big fucking deal*) but each time I talked to someone who knew what they were talking about, and I knew they were no more than a couple hours away.

Eventually, when everything we loved became mainstream and 'globalization' happened, shit became outsourced. That's fine, I suppose, because that"s a business decision and money is everything. And tied to that *exact* logic, if there were thousands of these call centers, then there were tens of thousands of call center *jobs*. Jobs = money. Money = women. It only made sense that these jobs, no matter how terrible, became convenient and attainable. After all, all you needed was a mouth and at least one eye to read the screen. Those are some truly reasonable requirements for full-time employment that didn't involve physical labor (which my dad wouldn't allow me to partake in).

At the end of my high school career or shortly thereafter, HP contracted out a call center right by where I lived, which was also close to high school (and incidentally college). They built this sardine can of a building where hundreds of automated humans provided tech support for HP's terrible home printers. Sadly, a few of those robots were my friends. I have nothing bad to say about their time there, and in fact, I might've been jealous. They were making bank while I was finding ways to scheme a buck here and there because I really wanted a PlayStation 2 and that shit be expensive to an unemployed enthusiast that spent all his money on his girlfriend(s) so he could get laid a few times a month and not get the clap.

Years passed and call centers became the laughing stock of all employment for educated people. The demand grew larger and yet the salaries shrunk, reducing the skillset to working at one to *merely being present when someone called in.* As the reality of being a freshly graduated dude with no experience or connections set in, we all entertained the idea of just working at a call center to get by (and get that Xbox and GameCube at this point). We had to - no one else was willing to give us a chance.

Educated, ready and willing but shit out of luck, that dark night finally came. I had just applied for 5 good jobs I wasn't qualified for, but it was time for a sixth - a Verizon Internet call center. Their job listing was appealing: Not minimum wage. Flexible hours. Benefits. Plastic keycard to show your mom. No physical labor. Being *downtown*, where presumably girls walked around wearing *skirts*.

Nervous, anxious and desperate, I sent my resume and cover letter, secretly praying that one of the other 5 jobs would pan out instead. After I hit *send* on my handy little Mozilla Thunderbird email client, I got chills when it hit me: I put the wrong fucking company name in the cover letter. Mortified by my irresponsibility and carelessness, I let my then-girlfriend enjoy my body while I lamented my actions. I could barely have a fourth orgasm while the mistake haunted me.

...none of that could've prepared me for what came next: *They called me for an interview days later.* Yes, they were so pathetically desperate for workers that a tiny thing like SENDING THE COVER LETTER MEANT FOR SOME OTHER FUCKING COMPANY - COULD EVEN BE MR. JONES' HEALTHY ANIMAL CARCASS CRUSHING INSTITUTE - didn't even affect my chances of getting the job. This was it for me - I was going to interview and get the job for sure. The bar was so fucking low that I would've cleared it by sitting on it. That's how I got *in*, and depending on who you ask... I never actually got *out*.

Zor:

Like all people who end up at a call center, mine came out of desperation for work. Actually, mine was worse than desperation. I recently quit a pretty decent job, was in college (for the second time) and was simply walking down the street en route to hanging out at said former place of employment. I had some bank, but finding a new place to work would be imperative to continue my non-existent high-roller lifestyle.

A block away from my destination, I ran into a high school classmate. While we weren't close, or barely hung out, we got along pretty well. He was having a cigarette break and told me all about his really "chill" work environment. After ten minutes of talking and building up how amazing this place was, he convinced me to send him my resume to pass along to his employers. **cue Simpsons reference: *"Can't a man walk down the street in this country without being offered a job?!"* **

Being young, stupid and desperate is such a horrible combination; I sometimes wish life would never curse us with all three at the same time. I sent in my resume that night with no cover letter. Understanding this is a call center, I didn't feel it necessary to take the application process seriously in any way. Well, lo and behold, they called me up for an interview three days later. I emailed a resume to an employee with no cover letter or accompanying application and still managed to get an interview. This was going to be good.

The interview became the beginning point of what would be the worst month of work I've ever experienced. They wanted to put me on a team that would provide wireless Internet support for truck stops across the US. And so the fun began...

Zor: Why Call Centers Fail the Formula

We included this chapter because we didn't want you thinking a job that is stupid easy to obtain and instantly gives you a paycheck would be an instant winner with our formula. It's not the case - at all. Let's look back at the formula:

Degree of Success = Results ÷ Effort

Results:

You either help a customer and they yell at you because "your" product is shit, or you can't help them and they yell at you because "your" product is shit.

Your paycheck barely makes enough to cover the rent and drink yourself to death.

Your co-workers spend all day long talking about how much they hate their jobs.

You're afraid to tell people you work in a call center.

A part of your soul dies every time you show up to work.

You feel defeated every time you leave work.

The best part of your day is abandoning your phone to take a dump... for 45 minutes.

I'm sorry, what results were you expecting when you work at a call center?

Effort:

It takes a crazy amount of effort to get out of bed and drag yourself to your job. Knowing you have to spend the next 8 hours listening to people tear a strip off you because the company you represent delivers shitty service takes a lot of willpower.

You have to trade in your dignity at the door, if you have any left. It takes a tremendous amount of willpower to not tell every person who calls you to "shut the hell up and read the damned manual!"

You spend all day long counting down the minutes until your break, then lunch, then quitting time.

If you get the night shift, it takes an inordinate amount of effort to get your body adjusted to the time-shift. The first few nights are hell because you can't sleep and you have to find ingenious ways to keep yourself awake at work.

You need to take a few breaths and summon every Zen-like practice you've ever heard of every time you pick up the phone.

The amount of effort required to work at a call center begins to reach critical meltdown when you leverage it against your personal health and well-being.

Degree of Success:

There is no degree of success in a call center. We haven't met a person yet who works in a call center and said, "Yes, I made it!" It's the second-last place you go for work because you just can't bring yourself to prostitution (and you're too homely for it). The fact v2 can get an interview when he puts the wrong company name in the cover letter and I can get in without even applying is a clear indication of their standards for employment.

Given the amount of effort you have to put into working at such a crusty place against the non-existent results you gain from it, the degree of success actually starts to leak into the negative. While there is no shame in receiving a paycheck, especially to support a family, we both understand call centers to be a result of desperation.

We walk in there thinking this is only a transition job, something to tide us over until we find something better. We never think we would stay there for extended periods of time. We don't ever consider call centers a place to make a long-term career. The turnover rate of call centers would also suggest that HR departments at these places know this as well.

However, when employment opportunities are scarce and nobody is willing to give you the time of day, your dream of leaving starts to dwindle. You begin to feel trapped knowing you have to remain here to make ends meet and there's no way to get out. Unless you get out early, this hope you have of leaving diminishes to nothing and you end up becoming a hollow shell of a human being.

To this we say to those working in one, **_GET OUT NOW!_**

The only degree of success we achieved as a result of working in call centers is v2's infamous "Verizon Exit

Interview." It still gets thousands of hits a month and even received a cease and desist order. It's too bad because "Dale" really needs to know what his daughter is up to when he's not around.

Choosing Your Friends

3-5 Friends are the Most You'll Ever Need

v2:

Friendship comes in several forms, most of which we'll promptly ignore in this chapter because they're totally false. There are precisely two types of friends: ones that are, and ones that are not. There's nothing in between. An *acquaintance* is exactly that, and a person you hang out with at work is a *co-worker*. Amazing, right? All that's left is an actual friend. You have very few of those and it's not a bad thing.

Following our formula, you must understand that you only have so much time and energy in your life. The fewer friends you have, the more quality each one must produce and absorb. Good luck entertaining 100 "Facebook friends" in 4 hours. You know what I could do with one real friend in 4 hours? Drive to Toronto, throw an Xbox 360 through a window of a call center, laugh, run like hell and make it all the way back to our hometown and still have time to get sushi ordered while we talk about our antics. For every friend you add to the story, you lose a little time. You lose a little enthusiasm. One "friend" won't laugh when the glass breaks. One "friend" will lament the loss of an Xbox. Add enough "friends" and eventually one of them works at the call center and was then tasked with cleaning up the glass. See where I'm going with this? Time and effort is linear and you can't keep splitting it up and still have a good time.

I'm proud to say that I have very few friends, but the friendships I have are clearly superior to how your little sister does it. For every friend that's come and gone, I pour a 40ozer to the ground and bid them farewell. I loved each and every one of you, but every one of your exits has added to the pool of appreciation and joy I have for those remaining. By virtue of mathematics, the friends that last are the best friends. Short of an actual funeral, you can't "lose" a best friend; the title only gets transferred to someone else.

When your parents, teachers and television (now supplanted by the Internet, I guess) aren't raising you, your friends are. You are, in fact, the product of your environment. I am everything my friends made me and they are everything I made them, insults included. You can't spend 8 hours a day at that impressionable age and not be influenced; it's simply not possible. It's because of Zor that I have a passion for videogames, because his library opened my mind to the exact things I *wasn't* playing at the time. I was rocking a Sega Genesis while he was rocking an NES, showing me the more cerebral side of gaming at the time with the likes of Zelda and Final Fantasy, games I didn't have access to. Likewise, another friend showed me the value of physical violence because violence is awesome. It helped me fight back against bullies until I became one myself, further helping my social life.

In my teenage years, I was introduced to Wu-Tang and became a better person. The same friend introduced me to stealing my dad's wine and going to the library while drunk and running into the glass doors. Another friend showed me the value of lying to women so they would talk to me despite my bad skin and laughable hair. At age 31, I am only a perfect summary of everything I've learned and I wouldn't change a thing.

None of these friends ever asked anything of me other than to drink a few beers or borrow their copy of hard to find video games

A real friend becomes a permanent pillar of your existence and it's not something that's interchangeable. I damn well know that there's no friend, current or former that can ever forget my ability to see the worst in every situation and say the most inappropriate thing possible. It's an art and it's what I bring to the table. It's the sort of ingrained thing that you can't learn from a virtual stranger.

Real friends don't require small talk or catching up. Friendship always fills in the blanks, so even if you haven't seen each other in a while, it's as if things continued right where they left off. You never have to bullshit or exaggerate because they'll know the value of your stories by your voice. Back in 2009 when I'd drunk dial my friends to tell them about a new girl (Jessica 2), they'd know I was serious because I was saying some serious shit (that I didn't care that her boobs weren't that big). They understood the power of my statements in the way that me telling my experiences to a stranger wouldn't convey. "You're an idiot, Tom," they'd promptly say. "Her boobs aren't that big and she has a *dog*. That's a deal breaker for you, so man the fuck up and bail immediately. Bitch ain't shit." That's what they told me and they were 101% right. Your real friends know you better than your own dick does - imagine that! It's sort of terrifying in the way that winning the lottery is terrifying to someone without the means to handle the change.

With everyone's opinion and information being consistent, everyone becomes valuable. You know that no real friend is going to sugarcoat anything and that no real friend is going to stay silent when you're publicly making a huge mistake in advance. That's the value of real friendship - a small, but powerful force that only ever does good for you. Choose wisely!

Sometimes you think that a friend has been lost because they moved away or you two drifted away. You're wrong! It's not possible! Those who you lose contact with weren't ever your real friends, just the same as how your first part-time job isn't and never was your career. Hurts, but it's true.

Zor: Why Some People Stay Friends Despite Moving Away and You Stop Talking to Those Down the Street

Growing up, you have fewer biases about the people you're willing to hang out with. You haven't been alive long enough yet for your parents to tell you why hanging out with the kid who lives in the dumpster is a bad idea. Nor do you have enough life experience to know the girl who keeps biting you in class is not the person you ever want to hang out with - ever.

It will only take you a few years in contact with other kids, but your worldview goes from enormous to a small narrow scope. You quickly discover the kids you get along with, the ones you don't but will still invite to your birthday because your mom made you, and the ones you're willing to give away your snacks to without trading anything in return.

As you get older, you solidify two things: your disdain

for change and your impatience for other people.

When you're young, friendship is built on very little and grows to be something you have for a lifetime. The older you get, the more friendship becomes a circumstance of convenience: "We're friends because we work together and get along," or "We're friends because our kids play together at school."

We move from finding the friends we'd be willing to replace our family members with to people who help us alleviate boredom. Of course they're playing along too because it's the polite thing to do. It becomes difficult to establish the bonds of friendship you had as a child, filled with secret codes, inside jokes and passwords.

While it's not impossible to establish friendship as you get older, it gets exponentially tougher. You connect with a lot more people but only focus on the few you've already put an effort into. Let's take a few examples to illustrate this point:

Example A: Frederick is a social butterfly and spends all his time trying to hang out with as many people as possible. He makes it a mission to keep his contact list filled with at least 400 people, all of which he considers "friends." Every weekend he sends out a mass message to his contacts to figure out what everyone is doing and slot himself in wherever there is availability. All the people he hangs out with consider Frederick "a friend who hangs out with us from time to time."

Example B: Gina has a small circle of friends she's known since high school. Every Wednesday night is ladies' night with no exception. When Gina moves away, her friends make sure to Skype each other once a week to discuss the subtext of shitty movies they've seen recently. Whenever Gina is back in town, all of them make plans to get together and continue the routine they've had since high school. They still plan trips together as if the distance they live has no interference in the logistics.

In Example A, nobody is really sure if Frederick considers them his close circle. They all assume they're a one-time deal and never get close to him because they just don't know if he wants to get close. Gina, on the other hand, still hangs out with other people in her new city, but doesn't make them a priority over the needs of her friends back home.

When you really sit down to think about it, you really only have 3-5 really close friends. These are friends who will never leave your side, always call you on your bullshit and stand guard while you piss in an alleyway. You really don't need any more friends beyond those ones because they get you.

You may be wondering why the people you've been talking to recently don't put the same effort into hanging out, or why recent friendships have gone stale. There's just not enough time and energy to go around to every person you meet.

The people down the street you hung out with every Sunday for a BBQ are going to get busy and will only make time for their older, more established friends. The friend who scattered across the country will still meet you online Sunday morning to build food farms for his Persian elephants, while your Korean War Wagons ravage the map (Age of Empires II - get the game and you'll understand).

It's hard to establish a history of memories, inside jokes and drama in such a short amount of time. Stop killing yourself trying to do it. There's a difference between being social and being a friend.

It doesn't take much to be social, but it takes everything out of you to be a friend... especially when he's slept with two of your ex-girlfriends.

Relationships

Because if you're actually any good, someone might
want to spend time with you

Zor:

I had some trepidation about writing the introduction
to this chapter, based on v2 being better with relationships
and having more experience in the women category.
However, his concern for my own romantic life and
timeless wisdom got me here today. It's from him I learned
how to be awesome when it comes to women. Well, better
than mediocre, anyway. The tipping point came in 2008.

We're sitting on the beach in California enjoying a
summer vacation - one which set the bar for all future
vacations. I told him about this girl I had an interest in and
let him know I was going to date her in the coming year.

Fast forward five years: v2 is standing at the altar as my best man. None of it could have been possible without the history we both had with relationships.

You may be wondering how our formula fits into this chapter. After all, if success = results ÷ effort, what does that say about the relationships we've had and the women we've been with?

Let's get the obvious out of the way. Relationships take a lot of effort. They take a lot of time and they don't always produce great results. You may think this negates the formula, but you'd be wrong. The *type* of effort you put into relationships determines your overall success.

I want to use three examples to illustrate my point.

The first example comes from the world of "pickup artists." I can't imagine a bigger waste of time... sorry, waste of *life* than to participate in the drudgery of that world. These guys spend all their time figuring out "strategies," "tactics" and "lines" to pitch to women in order to generate interest. Let's say this crap actually works and a girl feigns some interest. Then what? The girl didn't fall for you, she fell for your bullshit. You now have to spend even more effort keeping up the act and relying on your tricks and tactics to keep you going. It gets tiresome with each successive date and within a week, she realizes you're only a one trick pony and drops you.

The second example is the guy who tries way too hard. This guy spends all his time trying to please the girl he's interested in by being a mindless follower. She likes dogs? Now he likes, no... *loves*, dogs. She's into Cruel Intentions? He'll watch it a thousand times just to be able to quote it to her and hope she likes him for it. She asks him to buy her a sandwich and he'll fly to France to get her favorite one. He spends the rest of his time being a miserable zombie trying to keep up with everything she loves, but he'll do it because he's finally getting acceptance and love from someone.

The third example is a guy who is comfortable in his own skin. He knows who he is and doesn't have time to deal with people who don't interest him. When he meets a girl, she knows right away she's getting the real deal. She easily picks up on his values and understands what she's getting into the second she meets him. Not once does he feel he has to change when he's with her, but he'll put in an effort to change for the better when he's around her.

You may not *like* guy number three when you meet him and that's fine. At least you know that from the beginning. Not once does guy number three compromise himself in order to make a relationship work. The effort he puts into a relationship is focused strictly on the relationship, not on keeping up any pretenses about himself. Which one of those three achieves the highest level of success in a relationship?

To be brutally honest, if you can't do something that we're biologically programmed to do *naturally*, you probably suck as a human being. But that's okay because this chapter is all about how to stop sucking.

v2:

My stance on relationships is quite rigid I've had enough of them to form an educated opinion. I've dated pretty much every variation of women you can think of (except the types I haven't dated, of course) so I know what the deal is.

Right to the point: Plug in the formula. How much effort? How much success?

If it's difficult, it's not working. If it's not working, it's not worth it. If it's not worth it, why the hell are you doing it? To get laid? To feel acceptance? Don't answer those... they're rhetorical.

Being in a shitty relationship to get laid is the same as eating food when you're not hungry: It's of no real benefit to anyone. You can get laid when you're single. You can be in a good relationship and get laid. You can never get laid when you're single. You can be in a good relationship and never get laid. It's one of those things, and not one thing is mutually exclusive.

So yeah, relationships. The key to success is simple - find the right person for you.

That's it.

If it takes work, you will fail. If it's difficult, you will fail. If you have a lot of questions, reservations or concerns... it will fail. Couples who stay together for 30 years don't just have magical amounts of patience or strength - they simply have the right person. Swap out their partner with Kim Kardashian and they'd last 73 days or some shit.

My first serious girlfriend (let's call her... *Allison*)... man, I told her that I'd marry her. Told her we'd be together forever. Told her nothing could come between us. Couldn't picture being with anyone else, ever. All of a sudden I catch her cheating on me and we drop each other like the second Evanescence album.

Next girlfriend, same feelings. *2GETHER 4EVER* and all that. Bam. We break up.

Next girlfriend, same shit.

Rinse.

Repeat.

An entire decade later, I made a harsh exit from a nearly 5-year relationship. It was a brutal time in my life, for the only thing that made it reasonable was that I learned something very important: *This should be fun. This should be easy. The woman should actually like you.*

I started dating again, but this time picking from a different pool than I experienced before: Women over the age of 25 that were single. Why were they single? What's wrong with them? They actually have careers? They live on their own? No more having spontaneous sex the moment their parents leave to go grocery shopping? WHAT IS THIS MAGICAL WORLD?

I went out with more women than I am willing to admit (8 of them) but holy shit did I learn some amazing stuff right away. Please don't laugh at the following list, because I fucking guarantee at least one of these things will amaze you:

There exist girls that have their shit together.
None of this "still in school, working on my masters of bachelors' doctorate" or "in between jobs" or "saving up to move out of my parents' place" crap. Honest-to-god "I work in the marketing department and I pay the mortgage on my shitty little house and I own a white Toyota." My first date with one of those women was fucking thrilling. I used the phrase *MY PLACE OR YOURS?* and it was actually a thing. Before a certain age, you won't meet one of these girls. You just can't.

Girls, once they get past the "experimental" phase, can still be a lot of fun.
This one surprised me. Girls that were former wild and crazy tarts can sometimes grow into people that don't have a wild streak to them. Instead of getting more boring, per se, they get more interesting in a more subtle, complex way. The only thing I like to hear more from a girl than "*I*

love to make out with other girls" is "*I tried it once and it wasn't for me so I'm not going to do it and please don't offer me money to do so.*" There is a power to being in control of your emotions and it takes a certain maturity to do so. That's hot. More importantly, they take this open-minded thinking and use it to be more productive. This one girl I met went from "I tried to fuck every type of guy" to "I like to try new kinds of food, so let's go somewhere we've never been." It was awesome and really helped my irrational fear of contracting Hepatitis J from her.

It's actually possible for a girl to like you for you.

This one's cliché, right? It is, but there's also a deeper level to it. There are two sides to every man: The person alone in a room, and the person who interacts with people. Depending on what you're like, no woman is EVER going to like you for the weirdo you really are. That's OK! Realistically, let's take me for example. Given privacy, I do some stuff that would repel the very most desperate women. That part may be you, but you can keep that shit to yourself. You don't need every waking brain function to be shared in a relationship. That's why people need space. If you don't have space, you will be convinced that you will never find a girl who likes your poorly-painted Warhammer figurines. You won't find her. If you do, she'll be the girl who despises your shitty taste in movies. You are actually opening yourself up to failure! It's the equivalent of purposely annoying someone. Are you really expecting women to fawn over your worst, most embarrassing traits? If not, stop putting them front and center. Put your most humanistic side forward for them, and keep the personal shit to yourself where it belongs. I'm not saying to keep shit secret, I'm just saying that you shouldn't flaunt things that could/would repel a mate. You'd be surprised how many people do the opposite and bring out their worst traits right away to "test bitches" or "make sure she's crazy like me." Keep doing that and tell me how it turns out, mmmkay?

We are a product of our experiences, and our experiences are not the same.

This one's a doozy. One person hates dogs because they got bit by one. One person loves dogs because they protect them from being bitten by other dogs. As you date, you'll learn that not all long-term relationships start or finish the same. While casual dating, I spent a lot of time repeating, "Oh yeah... I been there!" to the shit I was hearing from girls. However, since I don't know the 15 stories before the current story, perhaps their experiences were nothing like mine. You can't assume that you're so relatable. You're not unique but you're also not the same as anyone else. The faster you figure out that you're not psychic and know everything about someone from dating them for a few weeks, the better you'll be. Love may be at first sight, but it's hatred that lasts forever.

Some people are fundamentally broken. You are not their mechanic.

You will or already have run into someone that's so screwed up that you'd like nothing more than be able to "fix" them. You can't fix someone, you can only help them cope. It's not your job to prevent someone from offing themselves. It's not your job to help someone out of debt. You are not a fix for someone's depression by showing up with Chinese food. People can heal and improve themselves only from within, over time and with inner strength. Let me save you a step - get the fuck away from these people. The negativity will destroy your life and what you think of others. I cried the shit out of my tear ducts for some bitch who had it rough with her parents and she was suicidal, etc, etc. By trying to help her, I had to be put on medication, fucked up my entire thought process and I hated women for years. All for what? A romantic hug in the rain? Wasted effort. Let someone else (someone stupider!) take the bullet for you. Try that girl in 10 years - if she's not dead, she'll be pretty decent. These things have a way of working themselves out.

If it's too good to be true...

you're an idiot. Attraction, love and lust are truly blinding things. I went out with girls who enchanted me with certain qualities (blonde hair, cash money, good hipto-waist ratio, fun) to the point where I was seriously not upholding my own value system. I hate dogs. I hate dogs more than you'd hate writing an essay using White-Out on 97 Brightness copy paper. I swear to you this is true: I was just about ready to move in with a girl that had a dog. Months later, exact same thing, except this dog was even bigger. What the fuck was I thinking? Hot ass and money, respectively. "Too good to be true" only exists because you're not seeing all the sides. Nothing can be *too good*. The problem with it is that if you actually look at everything, you'd see it's *no fucking good at all*.

...and lastly... and most importantly...

The right person for you actually exists. She married some other guy while you were wasting your time with someone else. Luckily, there's another one just like her!

There is no "the one," there is only "a good one." With effort, timing, luck and opportunity, the right person for you is right around the corner. They are not who you expected, not like you imagined and they think the same about you. You two will make things work because neither of you is going into it with such weird expectations and rhythms. Your favorite album of all time is one that you didn't really enjoy or appreciate the first time you heard it. That's how relationships work. Be open to not every piece fitting together perfectly and you'll suddenly realize it's a collage and not a jigsaw puzzle.

Holy shit that sounded poetic. Someone's going to steal that, make millions and put our formula to good use.

That's it.

Oh, and also, a hooker is cheaper than paying for date-night over and over again when the girl clearly doesn't like you. Given enough time, you might get lazy pity sex where she quickly runs off to text someone else about the horrible shame she feels. Not worth it.

In the words of Zor (and the great sage he learned it from) - "A hotel room is cheaper than a change of address." Don't bring crazies home. Crazies belong in a hotel room or in a bathroom stall. Keep them out of the sunlight or they'll be asking for child support in no time flat

Zor: Asking Her Out

No-Brainer Method: She asks YOU out because she wants you that bad.

Problem with the Method: Are you an A-list celebrity? How about B-list? No? Then it isn't going to happen so stop dreaming.

Easiest Way: A friend hooks you up on a blind date, or brings a friend to a group gathering for you.

Problem with this Method: You never know what

you're going to get and you have no say in the matter.

The Semi-Easy Way: Stalk her incessantly until she gets fed up with your antics and gives you a pity date.

Problem with this Method: Being labeled as a 'creeper,' a restraining order from the police and getting your ass kicked by somebody bigger and tougher than you. In the grand scheme of things, not recommended.

A Normal-Difficulty Way: Online dating.

Continuously stalk profiles until you see one that stands out, then make contact. You'll have to be clever to get the person's attention.

Women who do online dating receive hundreds of requests and messages every day. Pick one thing from the 'like' section of the profile and use it in the subject. Don't come off needy and desperate, just send a message to say you saw her profile and she has your attention.

Send enough back-and-forth messages to set the vibe you're the real deal and you're not using some automated script. Once she gets you're not acting out of character, ask for the date. If you're a half-decent writer, this shouldn't take you too long. If you're still messing up you're and your... it might be a while, unless she's just as dense and doesn't notice (or care).

Problem with this Method: It moves a lot slower and when you meet in person, you'll be starting from scratch again.

Normal to Hard: You approach her one-on-one and ask her on a date.

There are no "secrets," "tricks," or "magical pick-up lines" that will help you on this method. Just like every other man in history, you're going to have to suck it up and pull the trigger.

The only suggestion to making this work is confidence. Don't fake confidence to the point where you come across as an arrogant asstard, or you'll have bigger issues to deal with later. Don't overthink it, don't over-analyze - just do it.

Just don't sound like a moron when you do it. This includes babbling, trying to be funny or trying to come off like a ladies man when you don't even have enough wherewithal to know dousing yourself in Brut isn't sexy.

Problem with this Method: Fear of rejection. Sorry, no getting around this one. Not every person will say yes and there's no way to get rid of the fear. It can be minimized, but that's about it.

Hardest Method: Being a "Pick-up Artist."

You spend all your efforts trying to entice random women in clubs or on the streets. While your opening gambits and clever "lines" might get you in a conversation, where do you go from there?

When you step into this world, you're running someone else's game. How far you make it depends on how well you can be a fake version of yourself.

Problem with this Method: Women are pretty keen to this world of fake "ladies' men." I have a better idea - be an interesting person.

v2: The First Date

This is going to sound like terrible advice but I assure you that I have a method to my madness. On a first date you only have two goals: to do your best, and to immediately filter out the unwanted. That's it - every other pursuit is a waste of time, energy and money.

I always keep the first date simple. You want to do as much talking as humanly possible so you can learn about each other. You're going to be polite, attentive and patient. However, you're also going to be comfortable, logical and open-minded. Throw out some lesser-known facts about yourself. Tell her some mildly personal stuff just to see how she reacts. You don't want to wait too long to tell her that you hate dogs. You don't want to tell her that after you "meet" her dog, or whatever the fuck that means. Don't sugarcoat your opinions because it's only going to backfire later. If she's properly antagonistic, she'll do the same and you'll start to see the chemistry in the air. Disagreeing is more fun than idle chit-chat, at least as long as you're not discussing deal breakers, like how you *really fucking hate dogs* when she has nineteen of them.

As far as places go, going for dinner is a classic. You'll

get to find out if she can use chopsticks or if she's a lazy, ingrate forker. You'll see how she eats and immediately establish her attitudes about you paying and what she'll order knowing it's being paid for. If she orders lobster on your tab, send her home in a cab in the bad part of town. If she orders a burger and then pays for her own share, take her for ice cream afterwards. You'll know respectable behavior when you see it!

Next, do more talking. A walk, perhaps, or go see something touristy. There's a decent chance there's something common that one of you hasn't actually seen and you can work with that. (That's how so many of my dates ended up in a forest at midnight.) After the police found my beaten, robbed carcass, it was sort of a romantic scene. As long as you bring pepper spray and have good hearing, there's a good chance she won't have you taken out at knifepoint. I really should stop going for walks in my part of town. Shit ain't been the same since 9/11.

And finally, by the end of the night, you damn well know how it went. If you're getting a vibe that's less than one hundred percent positive, don't expect to ever see her again.

That's OK! Why continue seeing someone when it's not awesome? It's like test-driving a car and not really enjoying it - you don't have to buy it! It works both ways and no one should compromise or work at something that's shitty. When there's magic (or a reasonable facsimile) you'll know it. You don't plan a second date - it's already been arranged through your conversation with a million subtle hints and jabs. "Next time I'll kick your ass at air hockey!" is a second date. "I like eating here..." is *not*. Don't delude yourself into thinking it's better than it really is. Reality will tell you and it's best to figure it out beforehand!

Of course, like all living beings are compelled to, things will eventually become physical if you two hit it off. Here are some situations when you need to have a little control.

When to Say 'No' to Sex

Depending on who you ask, it might even be a funny idea that a man would ever say no to sex. Since you're asking me, I'll tell you that it's of prime importance that we say no as often as we hear it ourselves. There exist women that actually enjoy sex and even initiate it (!) and those are the exact women we must turn down just to bring balance back to the force.

There are many reasons why a woman would want to have sex with you. I'm going to explain them all so you can make the right call when the time comes.

She thinks you're super-hot and can't help herself.

You're definitely wanting to say no at this point, if only because, well... let's be honest here: How many hot women did you want to have sex with and they turned you down? Exactly. Saying no to a woman who is trying to get a purely physical thing going is giving every good dude you ever met a high-five. It's the right thing to do.

She's in love with you.

Probably OK to have sex. Watch out for babies, though - women in love tend to want to make more joy and that shit's expensive. If in doubt, say no.

She's doing it for revenge against a dude that wronged her.

Definitely say yes to this. If you say no, she'll find someone else, robbing you of what is likely to be a great experience. You can't really lose here. She won't talk to you after anyway, so you can tell her all about your Sega collection and not fear her ridicule of you not owning *Burning Rangers*.

It's her first time and she's curious.

Definitely yes to this, as long as you can handle the aftermath of emotional hilarity that will follow. Usually not too bad, especially with how bad a job you're going to do anyway.

She's desperate.

Definitely say yes to this. Think of all the times you really wanted it and would take anyone who was willing. Be a team player - make someone's day.

She's someone else's.

Definitely no on this one. Nothing good will come of this. At best you're going to get your ass whupped by some big bastard and at worst you're going to lose a friend because you're doing god-knows-what to his wife.

She's a freak.

Another no. A girl that wants to bang everyone all the time is probably serious bizness. Suggest one of your friends who doesn't have the class or restraint that you do; you'll get friend-props while deflecting the danger.

Having the ability to say no to powerful, hormonal feelings is what separates us from the animals. As soon as you're man enough to flip the script you become a higher being. People always want what they can't have so saying no is really the best way to ensure a resounding YES later on. The best sex you're ever going to have is when you work your ass off for it and you should always assume that it'll be worth it. Control is power, and it's nice to have some power at all when your peers are running around like dumbasses trying to touch anything that stands still long enough to intercept.

Zor: When It's Time to Commit

After all that work you've been putting into meeting her, doing the first date, attempting to be a superstar and trying like hell to repeat the process, the big decision comes:

How do you decide if this relationship is worth it?

Your values align and the two of you actually like each other.

To expect things to be perfect is like asking science to desalinate all the ocean water in one go. I'm sure there is a possibility of it happening, but that possibility only exists in science fiction books. There's always going to be personality quirks that will drive you up the wall.

Part of the challenge of a relationship is learning how to grow together. This is why I add the caveat of having your values aligned. If the two of you have been dating each other and growing in different directions, your relationship will go out of sync. If you try too hard to change the other person, you'll end up destroying what you initially liked about the person in the first place. Keep in mind if you didn't like much about the person to begin with, a warning bell should be going off in your head. The process of growing together should come naturally, not forced.

There will be days when you wake up in the morning and want to smother the other person with your pillow. Don't feel too good about yourself, though, because she's thinking the same thing about you. However, if your values are in the same place and you go to bed at night knowing you like the person you spent the day with - it's time to commit.

I can't give you an approximate time frame of when you pass the honeymoon phase and determine whether this is really working or not. As you get older, and hopefully more experienced, you have a better idea of what you want and don't waste time moving on with your life.

Once you determine the relationship is working and the two of you are happy together, make the next step sooner rather than later. Otherwise, you'll spend forever looking for the "perfect time." It doesn't exist and I want you to hear that now rather than realizing it 20 years later when you're waking up alone in a dingy basement apartment and every girl you had a chance with is in a happy relationship, making fun of your sorry ass.

The Wild Ride of Zor and v2

It would be a shame to leave this chapter without leaving you with a good story. This is why we're going to give you a half-decent story full of trauma and excitement (depending on who's telling it). In order to protect the identity of the parties involved, and thereby preventing us from getting sued for slander... or whatever fancy law term gets thrown our way... we're going to title this particular story, "The Story of Neve."

Zor:

I started dating Neve during my last year of high

school. She was great, I adored her and we even went to prom together. v2 didn't like her all that much and the two of them got along about as well as Syria and the US (too soon?). Nevertheless, I thought she was great - not to mention an amazing kisser.

I wouldn't know anything beyond the kissing, which became my downfall for this relationship. My late-teen self in all his naivety didn't see the end coming. I thought things were great. She didn't. The relationship ended just before the summer hit.

Did I sit around feeling sorry for myself? Hell no. I was upset, but I wasn't going to sit around all night crying myself to sleep while listening to *Our Lady Peace*. In fact, the night she dumped me we were supposed to go to a work function at a comedy club.

Right after I got off the phone with her, I called up my other good friend and invited him. It was an awesome night. Comedy clubs are a constant reminder that no matter how shitty things can get, a comedian can always make you feel worse about humanity - then make you laugh about it. By the end of the night, I had a good laugh and decided to join my co-workers at Everquest. It would fill the void of my former date nights.

By the end of the summer, I didn't think any part of me cared anymore about the emotional investment of the relationship. After all, it started in high school and now high school was over. It was a time of change, transition and moving on to other things. I thought I was good, until one fateful day in Toronto with v2, he turned to me and asked,

"Would you be upset if I dated Neve?"

I thought he was joking. He wasn't.

v2:

Before I'm labeled a friendship pariah, I feel the need for some facts to come out, #REALTALK. The following section in italics can be totally skipped as it's confusing for outsiders and only proves that I'm full of excuses. It totally sounds made-up.

That summer, I dated this girl named... "Katherine" and Neve was her best friend. Katherine and I broke up because she left me for my scumbag friend "Steve." I did not know this and I thought the break-up was organic. Like an idiot, I continued to chase Katherine all summer long while my friend Steve was seeing her. Steve and Katherine decided that the best way to get me to fuck off was to distract me with Neve. Neve agreed to their plan so she showed fake interest in me and I started thinking about her a whole lot. We saw each other at group functions and we seemed to be hitting it off. Their plan, unbeknownst to me, was working perfectly. Wanting Neve really made me forget about Katherine. All of a sudden Neve was hotter than Katherine because she didn't break my heart.

When the idea of dating Neve came up (because it actually seemed possible) I thought long and hard before proceeding. Being a decent friend, I sprung it on Zor. "Would you be upset if I dated Neve?" I asked, briskly shielding my face from the impending punch. I asked him while we were in Toronto to watch WWE Raw, so at least they wouldn't find my buried body as quickly as back home.

I can't say what went through Zor's head, but he basically gave me permission. I'll say this a million times and he might never believe me, but at the time that I asked him we definitely weren't dating. I was 109% entertaining the idea but I told myself that his decision would be final. Luckily, he agreed so I was all over it.

Neve and I started dating and it was amazing. She really *was* an amazing kisser. I fell for her hard (like, stupidly so, the same way when you saw Mario 64 for the first time in 1996). As the magic faded, the truth started to come out. She confessed that our relationship was a setup but that in the process she actually fell for me and she was 100% legit. Crushed and traumatized, I did the only sensible thing I could think of: take her virginity. I figured she owed me that much for messing with my heart. I'll always think of her fondly and that amazing summer. 2001 was, by far, the most memorable and significant year of my life, and my last year of being a teenager. It was the first time that I chose to be miserable instead of taking it easy. Most people don't choose that until their thirties so I was way ahead of the curve.

Neve and I ended in April 2002 after a break-ups and make-ups season that was exhausting and defeating. I might have tried to get her other friend into bed behind her back (fact). I might have tried to rebel against her mind games by getting with any girl that would have me (fact). She started dating someone else so it was final. So, in the end, was it worth risking my friendship with Zor to date this immature girl whose sole purpose was to break hearts on the regular? No, I guess not. Luckily we made it past that. She took a lot of things from me (pride, time, effort, sanity) and I gave back what I could, virginity excluded. Oh well for her!

What's the moral of the story? Don't date an Irish girl? You can't trust any girl that plays Tony Hawk on a then-new *PSone* when the rest of us are rocking the original gray box, now dreaming of a PS2. I don't know why but it's wrong. Playing games on a *PSone* in 2001 screams "nouveau riche hipster scumbag" to me, a clear sign that she was a pretentious little heartbreaking monster that masterminded the entire plan to hurt best friends and endanger their entire life-long friendship because she knew we couldn't resist the appeal of a girl that could work a controller without moving it around or giggling the whole time. It was a trap.

How to Stay Friends

Find your Alpha 2

v2:

Street Fighter Alpha 2 is a videogame that came out in 1996. You can Wikipedia the shit out of all you want, and you should, since we're not here to teach you about every platform it's been released on and how wonderful the opening intro is.

Anyway, the game is a competitive 1-on-1 fighting game. After a lifetime of being competitive as friends in many facets, here was this perfectly distilled experience of v2 vs. Zor in infinite grudge matches in a meaningful, direct way. One could easily try to wax poetic about how this game symbolizes our friendship's nature of one-upsmanship and the male traits of dominance, but shit no, we really just like playing this game because it might be the one thing we have approximately equal skill at and it's always entertaining. When you factor in the 1996-to-today bit, it's obvious that it's one thing that has truly stood the test of time

Playing another game like it is like having your newly-murdered childhood puppy well-meaningly replaced by your parents with one that has "shiner fur," "more affectionate" or "less loading time between matches." It's not Fluffy and it never will be, Pops.

Like anything else competitive, there are four stages each combatant must experience:

1 - The Hype: Talking about the upcoming match far ahead of time, making wagers, pre-bragging and trash-talking in advance. You build up the match to be bigger than it could ever hope to be.

2 - The Preparation: We clean the controllers, wipe the old CRT down to a streak-free shine and adjust the volume to somewhere between deafening and cops-show-up. Final trash talk begins. Threats are made. Innocent bystanders weep from their anxiety.

3 - The Event: Strangely, often a quiet affair. Other than match-ending moves causing pain and celebration, most of the sounds in the room are controllers being abused in precise ways. This is when hype starts to fall through and trash-talk is either justified or becomes a liability.

4 - The Afterglow: No matter who wins, we both feel defeated. There is only one victor but we were so damn sure that both of us were going to conquer the other. Instead of being good sports, we immediately break things into two parts: a) "You just fucking wait until next time when I avenge my loss!!!" and b) "I humbly retire as champion, never to play again because you're garbage and there's no point in wasting my future arthritic hands on you."

Those of you who are astute just realized we described the cycle of sex with a new person as well, but we really meant that our 4-stage process is applied to anything you do in life that's exciting or worthwhile.

If you're not getting excited about something and not going through the emotions before, during and after, it's not worth doing, period.

Think of how many wasted hours, days, years and lives have been spent on meaningless crap. Now think about all the times you worked hard and succeeded harder because your heart was in it! Oftentimes with just the right attitude you can either succeed or *feel* like you did. For every horrible date I went on, at least I was on a date while someone else was sitting around crying about it. For every shitty beer I had, at least it was the *fifth* one.

With all friendships, find your *Street Fighter Alpha 2*. Find something you have in common and let it bring out the best and worst in you. The more you do it, the more meaningful it becomes. Let it be your rock, the one thing you can share while the world changes (and often crumbles) around you. Growing up, growing apart, marriages, school, jobs and receding hairlines: they all disappear the moment you get back to what makes sense. For some it's golf, for others it's robbing convenience stores. Find your stable connection and stick with it. To quote something I read in a book once: "You've got to get obsessed and stay obsessed." Stop doing things on a whim and following the flavor of the month. Life and friendships aren't about fashion or style – they're about choosing the right people and making it work with them. It won't work out with all, and in fact it won't work out with most, but those left must be protected and celebrated.

...but all of that doesn't mean you can't beat their ass once in a while, videogames or otherwise. That's why Zor and I also play Age of Empires II; because the only thing better than competing against each other is working together to fuck up someone else's shit when they think they're better than you. Pardon my eloquent English, but there's no other way to get the correct cadence across otherwise.

Posting Bullshit Articles on Blogs Until One Hits

Zor: List Posts on "Advice" Sites

If there's one thing we promise you on Tommy|Zor, it's honesty.

You may not agree with our honesty, but you can be assured you're getting our best every time we write. We've worked at our craft so when you read us, it's *our* voice you're getting. We also write on a wide variety of subjects because our alcohol-fueled thoughts can't be pigeonholed into any specific category.

There are also a large group of excellent writers out there who are enjoyable as hell to read. Unfortunately, there's a massive glut of piss-poor formula writers who couldn't write their way out of a grade three journal. You can usually find their by-lines under list-post articles. Bullshit "advice" articles such as:

10 Ways to Wake Up Better in the Morning
5 Tools To Make You Super Productive
7 Things You're Doing That Make You Look Stupid

If any of those sound familiar, it's because you've probably seen a variation of that article at some point. It takes little skill or effort to put together one of those posts and yet they're the most commonly read articles by a mass audience. They're skimmable, require no intelligence or thought to process and rarely call you to take action on anything in life. There's a reason why magazines set their watch by these articles every season.

In other words, they satisfy the formula for immediate results.

For a small stint in time, I wrote articles for a major online blog and they requested their writers make a few list posts. In the short term, the list posts get immediate results and drive traffic to a site like a new Miley Cyrus video. However, the other articles I wrote for them, which contained my unabated honesty, destroyed those posts in the long term. I still get emails and referrals as a result of those articles.

According to our formula, you would think writing these bullshit posts would be the key to having the longest term success with a website. This is where we need to explore the idea of success. If driving traffic to your website is the sole definition of success, then your easiest path is to provide free porn to all.

While we haven't gone down that path (yet), we write for the long term. There's no success in giving up our voice and the years' worth of words we've written to pander to some amateur style of writing.

Degree of Success = Results + Effort

I kept writing about shit which pissed me off on Tommy|Zor and several successes happened: found my voice, defined my writing style and had a celebrity magician read one of my articles. People reading the site hate me for what I say or love every word I type. Those who like to skim my articles and make comments without having read them get mercilessly harassed in the comments section.

If immediate traffic is the measure of success on a website, I'm failing the formula.

If, however, being authentic and having people love you for it is a bigger measure of success, then list posts can go straight to hell.

On that note - list posts can go straight to hell.

v2: Being Ranked A Top 50K Website

In life it appears that it's all about who you know. These people don't have to be famous or anything, but if they're able to be at the right place at the right time then it's going to be beneficial. Here's one way it happened for us:

Back in 2004, I started a little website called Tommy v2 Online that was hosted on my ISP's free servers. I wrote little comedy pieces, some as short as a page with some dumb pictures sprinkled in. I showed them to my friends and co-workers (huge fucking mistake — more on that in our eventual sequel!) and they started showing other people... you know how it goes. It wasn't viral, but it was airborne bacterial at least.

Eventually I bought myself a domain and hosting and put it up as a dotcom to hopefully gain more exposure, as well as not worrying about my ISP shutting me down for foul language or some shit. It was certainly nicer and my popularity grew to some extent. Back then, the ranting and blogging scene was incredibly tiny and if you were one of the, say, 10 people doing it, you'd be seen and heard. Time goes by and my writing keeps getting more and more elaborate, now with my articles spanning multiple pages with actual flow and a readable layout. I then had some job trouble and wrote my famous "Verizon Exit Interview" which caught on well (millions of hits if you believe the analytics of 2005) but it didn't really keep bringing people back to the site. One hit did not create the infamy I was looking for.

Like all things, I grew dissatisfied with my lack of Internet fame so I started being hard on myself and reflecting my misery in my work. Instead of being funny I focused on being shocking and exploitive, spiraling into nonsense until I was just writing about every little thing that bothered me, no matter how inane. At the height of my anger I wrote a little piece called *MySpace Ruined The Internet Like the iPod Ruined Music*. It was a sad little number, full of rage and hatred, and now looking back: prophetic. In the end it was one of those "no one's reading so I'm just going to go nuts" sorta things and went for broke.

Nothing happened overnight until it did: a friend of mine, let's call him… "Richard" (which is actually his name), decided to submit the article to one of those then-trendy content aggregator sites. He never said anything at the time, I casually looked at my traffic stats and could not believe my eyes. Tens of thousands of hits where there should be mere hundreds. Graphs spiking so hard you'd think it was Olympic volleyball.

And the best part? A lot of those people kept coming back for more. Finally, I was being appreciated and enjoyed for my writing. Like the spoiled brat I was, I kept delivering the goods several times a week and was, approximately, INTERNET FAMOUS. My e-peen had grown. I was getting fanmail (and more hatemail)! I was getting nudes sent to me! I was cool! I was meeting women who knew (of) me and wanted me! Two of them were totally physically attractive on top of having good taste in reading material! I touched boobs! *I touched the boobs of a stranger because I wrote stuff on the Internet.*

My website was ranked 33,000th *something* on the entire planet which was no small feat without the aid of viral social media.

A year after that I hit it even bigger with my most famous and meaningful article of all: *Facebook is the End of Humanity.* This was back in 2007 when Facebook was still pretty tiny and I already knew what the world would turn into. It was a huge hit but the telling thing is the longevity: it's still going strong and still as accurate as the day it was written. I didn't expect Facebook to last past 2010 (if that!) because to me it was just MySpace for grownups.

Like all good things (and fads), I just ran my site into the ground. I experimented with monetizing the site, violating every terms of service anyone could ever write. Thanks to fans and their rampant abuse, my advertising was shut down the day I finally earned something off the site. Deflated, disappointed and mad (that I got caught), I decided that site was no longer going to cut it for me. On top of growing up and no longer being (as) mad at the world, my personality started to slip off the pages and it became a chore to write. That was my creative death-knell: If it ain't fun, I ain't doing it.

Luckily this story has a part two, and that's when Zor and I decided to start a site together, fulfilling our childhood dream of writing together. Tommy|Zor was born and here we are. I don't know who and how, but I know that some of the original fans from 2004 onwards have stayed true to us, joining the few new fans we have. Now sadly lost in a sea of blogs and opinion pieces, we still find ways to stand out and stand up. All of those people who just skim and move on after a page or two looking for some magic that doesn't exist (spoiler: magic isn't real) are troubling. With roles reversed you'd flip if someone ignored your stupid Facebook status update about your brand new shoes that you ruined with your #YOLO stupidity.

Our dedicated fans have always been supportive. They've made our endeavors worthwhile because we know that someone out there is cracking a smile over a joke that took me all day to write. Being on the other end of the equation I've seen many great websites shut down, taking all their talent with them, never to be enjoyed again. No matter what you think of progress, growing up or boredom, at least we're around, approximately keeping it as real as ever.

Speaking only for myself, I know I'm no longer a young dude with a platinum Amex card bragging about how many Tommy Hilfiger shirts I own. I'm well aware that having a $7000 car does not make you certified BALLER STATUS! and that girls may not be impressed with my spiky hair with frosted tips. Fuck it, I don't even comb my hair anymore and any Hilfiger shirts I own are from the thrift store because they're the only ones that didn't have Hawaiian prints on them and cost $8 or less. My "macking on bitches" is now just grocery shopping with wifey and my beautiful face-only tan is likely from having a 30" monitor and using a lot of Microsoft Word without turning the brightness down sufficiently.

So, to all of you faithful, thanks for staying with us and enjoying what we do. To those of you who have left... well... send us some money or something. Buy this book several times. We have to recoup our hosting and domain fees since 2008.

You've made us successful because we barely worked for it. We enjoy and have fun doing it, and that ain't work. That's the formula in action. After all, I once worked really hard at a slave job and didn't touch a single stranger's boob from it. That's a formula failure right there!

Why Social Media Experts Can Go Away

Facebook IS the End of Humanity

Zor:

Let's take a look at the classroom of today:

"Susan, put away your phone and pay attention."
"Just a *second.*"
"I said now!"
"Oh my god – relax! I'm just finishing this message."
Teacher calls Susan out, sends her to office for truancy and tries to confiscate her phone on the way out. While

Susan has no problem walking to the office, she fights on the phone.

"You're not taking away my personal property!"

A part of the teacher dies knowing this type of behavior is only getting worse and there's nothing she can do about it. What was Susan doing that was so important?

Snapchatting, messaging, Twitter feeds and Facebook updates... because... you know... for a 14 year old, something interesting is always happening to your friends every second of the day. Thus, the paradox occurs. Susan is one of many who spend all day looking at what other people are doing because she has to measure accordingly against her own life. Don't ever tell people like her it's an insecurity issue either, unless you want to watch someone become defensive to the umpteenth power.

With the proliferation of cheap data plans and ease of access to smartphones, the plight of spending every waking moment checking your phone for updates is upon us. People are either checking for updates, "checking-in" as an update, providing an update, or checking to see if someone has responded to an update.

There's a reason v2's article, "Facebook is the End of Humanity" is still the most popular article on our site. Hordes of people read it daily and it goes through bursts of getting discovered by small masses of people who are sick of social networking. These are people who are sick of their "friends" continuously editing their lives in order to show a version of themselves, which is only partially true or not even close. According to social media: people have perfect relationships, vacation all the time, are inspired 24/7 and are all raising the perfect children. Everyone is also dedicated to social causes because they re-post/re-tweet/share some update about some event happening... because we all know clicking a button on the Internet and adding a comment will make change happen.

Then there are those who attempt to use social media as a "platform" for their business. They obsess over their klout scores (size of network + what people do with content posted = influence). "More followers! More people! Higher score!" Try explaining to these people the people with the highest klout scores are people who have done something in *real life* and just happen to be on social media.

It's now at the point where posts and responses don't even make sense. It's as if the interesting people of the world all left the Internet, and all we're stuck with are hordes of boring people attempting to make their lives sound so interesting and profound. All you have to do is post something like, "Woke up this morning and my hand was numb."

Wait for the responses.

How Things Have Gotten Worse and Why Social Media Should be Used as Dating Sites

One of our favorite articles in the history of Tommyv2 and TommyZor is "Tommy v2 Does Online Dating."

Before the influx of social networks, dating sites were the original horde of people posting dishonest profiles in order to get other people's attention. If you read carefully, you could interpret the profiles to get a good idea of what people were *really* saying. Then there were the brutally honest profiles, which got the attention of v2.

It was a simple endeavor – you posted a profile, waited to connect to someone and gave up when nothing happened. The smart/good looking ones would leave after too many hits to their profile. It was a perfect equilibrium of people joining and leaving, with the desperate ones who lingered on in hopes of something happening.

Unfortunately, social media has gone from bad to worse. There is no equilibrium. In exchange for having a free place to post your "inspirational quotes," and aggregated content – the companies who run these sites have now allowed businesses to advertise in your space. Congratulations. You managed to bring back banner ads in an intrusive way. Not that peoples' content is worth looking at anyway. It's not even about sharing anymore, or connecting with others, it's about attention. Everyone is screaming, "Look at me! Look at me!" and they have nothing interesting to provide in return for the attention.

It's sad: millions of people connecting together with nothing to say to each other.

What was the original intention of Facebook?

To start an exclusive digital fraternity in order to meet girls.

Let's go back to that.

What Does This Mean for Our Formula?

The so-called "social media experts" are nothing more than experts at bullshit. Can you really train people how to make friends? Dale Carnegie tried this years ago with the "How to Win Friends and Influence People" book and seminars. In essence, he was the first social media expert... except he was talking about real people... making real connections.

What do current social media experts offer you exactly?

For a small "consulting fee," (code for, "Get ready to re-mortgage your home") they will help you expand your influence and build a "legion" of followers. What the hell is a legion? It's a fancy way of saying, "an indeterminate amount, avoiding anything specific as to give myself a loophole when my bullshit proves it doesn't work."

The idea of spending all your time building your "social media presence" also fails our formula in a large way. You spend all your time on a medium that doesn't actually do anything for you. Honestly. Posting your breakfast foods, complaints, "insights," and links to other peoples' content doesn't do anything to help you. All you're doing is spending all day telling people to look at you even though you're not doing anything interesting.

If you really want to apply the formula to your online presence, do the following:

Do/Create something awesome.
Share it.
If it doesn't go "viral," start over.

Don't waste your time finding the perfect background image, taglines, layout, or whatever other nonsense people will tell you will "help." If your shit gets popular enough, people will come to you with offers to do it.

Enough with the bullshit. If you want to increase your following, do something useful.

Getting Through the Front Door

Zor: Forget "Career Counseling" and "Networking Events"

I have a confession to make:

I've never gotten a job by applying for it through traditional means.

Every single job I've ever gotten has all been on the connections I've made from people who were already in the industry. I would still submit my resume and go for the interview, but they were pretty much formalities at that point. Well, not quite formalities because there was still a chance I could really screw things over, but it was almost a certainty.

I have epitomized our formula on the job seeking front.

Does this mean all my jobs were ridiculously amazing? Not at all, but I got them.

Aside from the call center, there was something I loved about every single job I've had. I worked for my buddy's dad, an Internet cafe, an automotive assembly line, a shoe store, a construction company, website design for a non-profit, teaching and a professional magician.

How hard do I work to make these connections?

Not all that hard.

I didn't take any Dale Carnegie courses on how to win friends and influence people. I didn't join toastmasters and I didn't weasel my way into groups just to make connections. I simply made connections with people, did shit that interested me and didn't burn any bridges with employers I eventually left. I also made some enemies because you can never get everybody to like you.

Really, it's not nuclear physics. It's the simple ability to *not* be an asshole to everyone you meet. Next thing you know, people are telling you about opportunities that open up. Does this mean I never have to hustle when I start work? No. If someone is willing to vouch for me, then I have to work extra hard so I don't make my friend look like a fool.

Make friends with people without expecting anything in return and work your ass off when they give you an opportunity. It works. You know what doesn't work?

Networking events.

Those are a complete failure of the formula. The usual breakdown of networking event is a mish-mash of people looking to get something for themselves (instead of offering something) and real estate agents. It's forced friendship. And the last thing you want after leaving school is being forced to make friends with people around you because there is no other option.

At best, it's an attempt at a shortcut in life.

Shortcuts, full of their tips and tricks, may get you ahead in the short term. But people will hate you in the long term. People know when they're being used. Once they get that impression about you, good luck. You disrupted the love/hate formula and you will suddenly find yourself the target of death wishes.

v2: The Actual Front Door Method

I have a confession to make: I only ever succeeded career-wise because I was awesome. If you believe in career destiny (hint: there's no such thing) then I must've had it. The first time I ever printed a resume and used my arms to hand it to someone who mattered, I got the job. I did it at the same time as someone with experience, someone who looked better (as if, right?), was older and generally better put together. I handed someone my first resume and that led to my first interview. Quickly that led to my first job and obviously my first firing, but that's another matter.

[Spoiler: I'm a lousy employee when it involves *actual* work].

I'm handy with words and well-spoken so my resume and interviewing skills tend to be impressive, at least compared to most people. That's really the secret here and where our formula applies: it's actually less effort to make an amazing resume that's bangin' than to constantly give out a shitty one that produces precisely zero results and wastes everyone's time. Your resume is your first-and-only impression you give. I suppose these days it's also your "cover letter" (aka email body which tells the employer you know how to attach a Word document) but I lump all that stuff together because they are a package. You want to make a good impression but you can't focus on one "dream job" because competition for anything good is always going to be stiff and there's small chance that you're not the best in the world at something.

Let's quickly recap: Do a good job because someone will always do better, but using the same amount of time you can get to more potential opportunities and therefore could actually succeed more.

For a selfish, ego-centric extrovert, I'm actually rather shy. I don't do networking events, I don't like meeting new people and I sure as hell don't like putting myself out there to compete with all the other loudmouth idiots looking for their time to shine. All my jobs have been the result of "traditional" methods - apply, impress, present and hang on for dear life, mostly in that order. Rejection is always part of the process but quitting rarely should be. Everyone has a certain amount of self-esteem they're willing to risk to get something done. Putting yourself out there and using your time to do it is always scary and should be treated with care and respect, so it's no time to be lazy or careless. To paraphrase something I heard: "It's funny how there's never enough time to do something right but there always seems to be enough time to do it over."

In terms of career, if you're going to be staying in the same field, you should always be looking to move upwards. The best time to get a job is when you already have one. It's just how women are all over me when I'm not single: there's a certain aura a human gives off when they are succeeding at something and it cannot be faked. Likewise in terms of moving upwards, the trick is to *apply for the job you want, not the job you already have.* I worked helpdesk and call center in my life... do you think that's on my resume? Not a chance. If they see that, then that's what they'll make me. I worked retail. Not on there. If you want to be a manager, talk about some management shit you did or something awfully close to it! It sounds silly but it's a common mistake. Some people treat their resume like a biography - and it surely ain't that. I went to a shitty school with a bad reputation and my first jobs were trash. Instead of dwelling on it, I just transcend my history and put my best foot forward. No one's second-guessing my crappy schooling once they see that I can write, held down several career jobs and presented my skills in meaningful ways. They *couldn't*. It just wouldn't make sense.

As my work years went on, I left great jobs for "better" ones - sometimes taking huge risks in doing so. I'm the same guy who bailed on a 5-year-long good relationship for "the dream" of meeting someone who I would want to spend *6* years with. Sometimes you become complacent and don't realize you could be doing better or you're actually not happy. That's no way to live life. Don't get me wrong, I'm no proponent of "Do what makes u happy!!!1" because then you're advocating to people to be drug addicts and child molesters. However, deep down you know what happiness is and how you could extract more by improving your own situation. That's our formula in play - make the small changes in life that bring the most total success to you, even if it's not immediate. I left a good job where I worked awesome hours and never answered a phone for another job that's immediately more annoying. Why? Because thirteen thousand dollars a year more buys a lot of video games and beer. That's the job that let me buy a house and own a PS3 for every room (almost kidding). It's the sacrifice I made and it paid off. Sometimes it doesn't, but that's part of the game. No risk, no reward.

In conclusion: either Zor's method of self-starting, knowing the right person and being at the right place and right time, or my method of putting yourself out there and risking countless anonymous rejections, it's going to work out eventually. What *doesn't* work is doing fuck-all nothing and expecting the world to hand you things because you're privileged and magical because your mom said so. That works for precisely two sets of people - children of the very rich and freak lotto winners. If you're neither of those, I'm afraid that today you are going to have to get off your ass and do something if you want to make life better. Sorry!

Zor: Teenagers Practicing Magic Will Rule Over Your Need to "Find Your Passion"

At the request of a friend, I watched the documentary "Make-Believe." It follows a bunch of teenagers around the world who are competing in the Las Vegas Magic Seminar: the worldwide teen competition for magic. If you have any interest in magic, the documentary is fun to watch.

If you dig a bit deeper, you discover something about these teenagers that most of society will never grasp. One of the kids competing in this documentary is only fourteen years old. He comes home, does his homework and practices magic for five hours a day - every day.

Another kid is from Japan and he made his own props because he couldn't afford to buy the latest magic products. He makes some of the most difficult sleights in magic look ridiculously easy.

One of them builds his own props and customizes it to

his show. No one else in the world has the same products as him unless they call him up and ask to buy them off him.

You know what they don't do?

Spend all day reading articles on "How to Be a Magician." They don't spend all day scouring websites on "tips and tricks" for "enhancing your performance." And they sure as hell don't read self-help books on the subject, trying to find their passion in magic.

They love magic, so they do it.

It's a lot of work, but by the measure of our formula they're ridiculously successful. They spend a lot of time upfront learning an act. They practice the act and then they take it on the road to go compete, earn money and travel the world showing it to others. Later on, they'll eventually tweak and add different elements and routines to their act.

Over time, the value of what they've done in the beginning stages increases exponentially. They also build skills that are transferable to any other discipline in the world: good with their hands, dedication to a goal and discipline to see it through.

The notion of finding your passion is ridiculous. It's only meant to pad the wallets of fake experts looking to take advantage of gullible people so they'll buy their products. If you like something, go do it. If not, shut up - no one cares.

...Sneaking Out the Back Door

Zor:

We get stuck in our jobs because of something else going on in our life: student debts, mortgage, rent, bail money for Uncle Jim, etc. If we like our jobs, or can tolerate them at the very least, this isn't too much of a problem. However, when you wake up every day and get anxiety attacks from thinking about work, there may be a serious problem.

What's the point of going into work every day if you always have a heart attack every time you make it to the front door? Is the paycheck from that particular company really worth the several mental issues you will have down the road, forcing you to not only quit your job, but never again be employable? Maybe I should pre-empt this section with the following before I continue:

There is no dream job.

There are jobs you love, jobs that get you excited, jobs that you tolerate and are ambivalent towards and jobs that you hate. If you have any of the first three, you're doing great in life. However, you need to get the idea out of your head that there's some magical dream job out there where every day is sunshine and roses... unless you're a horticulturist and that's *literally* your job.

Even when you're doing something you love, there are days when you'll doubt yourself. You'll wonder if this is really where you want to be right now and you'll wake up the next morning questioning why you loved it in the first place. Some jobs, on the other hand, are a trap. They'll eat you alive, grind you down and make you wish for a winning lottery ticket just so you can hire someone to stab your boss.

Sometimes, we get into a job we *think* we'll like and it ends up being a disaster. The worst thing you can do is pretend things will be okay because you will wake up every day and hate yourself a little bit more. You'll start wishing for other things in your life while crying yourself to sleep and bitching about it to your friends... all the time.

In those two cases, it's time to leave. Using our

formula, the amount of effort you put into a job that's stealing your life (results) puts your success in the negative. All your energy is being focused towards making it through the day rather than going home and enjoying your life. Your nights are spent trying to re-energize your mind only to have it sapped again the next day.

When you finally come to an awareness this job isn't working out, don't quit right away. Start the process of finding another job and wait until it pans out; then give your two week notice and leave. Don't burn any bridges on the way out, unless you sued someone in your workplace for something horrible, because you never know how connections work nowadays. The boss you told to go "fuck off," might be golf buddies with your new manager, or your girlfriend's uncle. I don't know, strange shit happens in life. Don't go burning bridges. Quit your job when it's time and don't cause a scene on the way out the door.

v2:

I'm no stranger to either quitting or getting fired. I was fired from my first job, which was wonderful: they saved me the trouble of quitting because it was the worst job I could have at that age. Me, doing physical labor? Oh, please.

As Zor said, if you hate your job, you have to bail. Being smart about it means that you move to a different job, forgoing the risk that it might actually be worse. Hope springs eternal and all that. It's infinitely (I swear I can mathematically prove this) easier to get a job when you already have one, just like how when you're dating someone, everyone else wants you, too.

Removing stress in a permanent way is one of the best feelings a human being can experience. The key word is *permanent*; simply masking stress only tends to build it up even higher. Leaving a stressful job is tantamount to watching your dangerous stalker get shot and killed by the cops. There will finally be peace, at least until the stress of other things (combined) start to fill the happy hole in your soul. Realistically, the sole purpose of any given job is to obtain money to buy shit you don't need and to support those people who could be better supported by someone else.

With that in mind, as long as money is coming in, life can't be that bad. To quote myself: "The only people who don't want to be millionaires... are billionaires." If your job is anything other than tragically horrific on a daily basis and you're getting paid more than you spend, you're in good shape. If not, you're doing something wrong and you're not using our formula. *Either make more money or spend less money.* It's not how much you make, it's how much you keep. It's really that simple. Do what you need to do to lower your job and financial stress. Check out this scientific anecdote: 100% of the happy people I know don't have money issues. I'm not saying they're rich or even have any decent money at all, I'm just saying they don't have issues with it.

Of course I went off on a tangent so I'll get back to it: Jobs are an unfortunate part of life for all of us. No job is as good as waking up at noon and drinking a Sam Adams. Beg, borrow or steal whatever guts necessary to be strong and not put up with a horrible job. A job can be one-third or half your entire day. Do you know what the remaining time has to be like for you not to want to jump off a cliff? Exactly. **Success = result ÷ effort.** Find out where you job fits into that and do something about it.

I Call Bullshit On Your Success Story

"Okay, here's the deal, I'm not here to waste your time. Okay, I certainly hope you're not here to waste mine, so I'm gonna keep this short. Become an employee of this firm, you will make your first million within 3 years. Okay, I'm gonna repeat that: you will make a million dollars, within three years of your first day of employment at J.T. Marlin.

There's no question as to whether you become a millionaire working here. The only question is, how many times over."

-Ben Affleck, Boiler Room

Zor:

If you haven't seen Boiler Room, go watch it now. For the quick version, do a video search for "Ben Affleck Boiler Room Speech."

The real point is anybody promising you success in the form of millions of dollars is either scamming you or getting you to help scam others. It was amazing to watch this movie and a few years later get suckered into a Primerica "Opportunity Meeting." I couldn't help but laugh at the similarities between the pep-talk I heard in that meeting versus the one Affleck gave in Boiler Room.

They went on and on about the people in the company who were making hundreds of thousands of dollars, some who made the millionaires club and how the dream is possible for just about anybody with enough ambition. At the very least, they were selling a legitimate product.

While Primerica itself isn't a scam, it uses an antiquated way of generating a lead: make a list of people, hunt them down and try to hard sell them your products. If you hate selling things to people, or really suck at selling, you will not succeed with this company. If you can't generate leads, you will also fail.

At least the people pitching you are actually legit with their own claims, which is contrary to what can be said about the growing number of "Rich Dad" seminars popping up across the country.

Let me break this down for you:

- Advertisement goes on the radio about a *free* seminar in the city to teach you about how to become wealthy off of real estate. It's the real deal too because it has the "Rich Dad" branding
- You show up to the seminar and the person talks all about how amazingly successful they've been. They'll even give you a sob story of how they were down to their last few pennies before applying these methods and now becoming super-rich
- Rather than continue being super rich and making millions, they want to teach you how to do it because they have a "genuine interest in helping others"
- Bait-and-switch
- To learn the "secrets," sign up for the $500, 3-day seminar
- You sign up for the $500 seminar
- Bait-and-switch
- The "actual, REAL secrets" are in the $30,000 training course
- Nobody learns anything and you were better off buying 50,000 shares of Farrowtech

CBC (The Canadian Broadcasting Company) did a take-down of one of these seminars. The guy leading it was not only lying his ass off about his own "investments," (which didn't exist) the methods he taught weren't true (or even legal) either.

On the surface, this sounds like a pretty obvious scam to many people. Yet, whenever the promise of a ton of money is made, there are always willing people to be suckered in to this nonsense.

And the promise of making money has been so rampant online, it's beginning to give me an aneurysm. However, I have to hand it to these people because they've mastered the dark side of our formula.

They want to make a lot of money, so they sell courses to people on how to make a lot of money. Just add a few lines such as, "results not typical," and "if you prove to me you've worked through my material and it doesn't work, I'll give you 100% of your money back." Then sit back and watch the profits come reeling in.

However, over the long term, the "results" part of the formula starts to become an issue. At the beginning, results are high profits from little effort. Having to copy and paste information from other source materials doesn't require a whole lot of work. As time goes on, having to change your identity and run from people who want to fire-bomb your house becomes a problem.

My personal favorites are those who claim to be "successful writers" and if you buy their course, you can learn how too!

Let's see...

J.K. Rowling generated over a *billion* dollars writing stories - you're not her.

Stephen King has sold over 350 million copies of his books - you're not him either.

Your name isn't Richard Dawkins, Elizabeth Gilbert or Malcolm Gladwell.

So who are you to be teaching about writing success?

Want to know why the above mentioned don't sell courses on how to be a successful author? They're too busy writing books people want to read. Take note.

As far as I'm concerned, any online success story is bullshit until proven otherwise. While the technology on the Internet has changed since 1996, the mentality hasn't. The Internet is still the greatest platform to lie to the largest group of people.

What Success Looks Like In 2014

Zor:

v2 and I are relaxing at Newport Beach in California. After I graduated University, we took a trip down to visit a friend of ours. Since being there, we got to fulfill a childhood dream of mine by visiting the Magic Castle. Earlier that day, we visited the pier where they filmed Arrested Development. My only disappointment was the non-existence of the actual frozen banana stand used on the show.

We spend the rest of the trip hanging out at the beach, eating frozen bananas and drinking at 7:30am (it's 11am *somewhere* in the world, not that it matters).

A few years later, we're back in California for San Diego Comic-Con. While there, we get Hideo Kojima's autograph, watch a panel with Nolan North and Emily Rose, meet the guys from Penny-Arcade and pre-empt our days by drinking at 7:30am. It's one helluva time!

The morning of my wedding, we drank at 7:30am, played video games before the ceremony and closed the night by dancing to *Jellyhead* by Crush. For my honeymoon, my wife and I went to an all-inclusive resort in Mexico where our biggest dilemma was where we were going to lounge that day. The bartenders knew my order before I even sat at the bar every evening.

When I first moved cities, the first people I met were other magicians. They taught me how to routine my shows and build a business out of it. I spent the next eight years taking a hobby I loved and doing something profitable with it. I never performed on a Las Vegas stage, but people still bug me to this day to show them another trick.

I also have a day job I love and spent the last five years being uncompromising until I got it.

I don't have a million dollars, or a 5000 square-foot home. I don't vacation on private islands in secluded parts of the world that are only accessible by helicopter. To me, the excitement would wear off when the island runs out of beer and there's nowhere for me to get more. A house may have fifty rooms, but you can only use one room at a time. My vacations to California are still the greatest memories I have with my friends.

You may never make a billion dollars, launch a rocket ship into space, discover the cure for cancer or write a New York Times Bestseller. Don't beat yourself up over it. Real success comes when you discover the definition to one word: **enough**.

How much is enough? If the answer is, "just a little bit more," you will never achieve any success in life. You will be plagued by always trying to compare yourself to others: the people higher than you at your job, your "friends" on Facebook who are always posting vacation pictures and random success stories on the Internet.

The world is rapidly changing and the measure of success has changed with it. Despite the doomsayers, we're living in a much superior time in comparison to those 150 years ago. Again, this brings us back to the question of how much is enough? Eliminate the words 'boredom' and 'worried' from your lexicon and that should do it.

Every day I wake up and realize I could scale up what I'm doing for even greater financial success. The thought quickly goes away when the realization sets in I wouldn't have a life outside of work. I wouldn't be able to watch Netflix Originals with my wife, plan gaming weekends with my friends, or just simply enjoy that I'm getting by doing what I do.

Zor signing off!

v2:

When it really comes down to it, success (in any form) is all relative. For most, "success" means getting to a goal, no matter how small. Today I "successfully" drove to work without crashing or killing another person and making orphans. That's a small thing, though, and it certainly scales from there.

To someone else, making $60 million bucks instead of $50 million bucks is succeeding. That, too, is scale; as *that* task may be easier for that person than it would be for you to put down new ceramic tiles in your bathroom. It all depends on your position in life and your universal importance to the world itself. Most of us make precisely 0% difference in the world to others, but that's OK, too. We don't have to be important, we just have to be useful to someone. We are truly "tools" for society. You might be a literal tool to mow lawns, but your employer is a tool to those with lawns to upkeep. That hotel chain is a tool to shareholders, and shareholders might just be dudes with money that also don't feel like mowing lawns and pay you to do it, or they're just regular people with a few extra bucks sitting around. There's no shame in being part of the cycle of modern life if that's the choice you've made. Your real choices are corporate slave, being homeless or being a monk. That's pretty much it. Choose wisely!

In this book we have explained and demonstrated different ways to succeed by focusing your energy in the right ways. With discipline and careful thought, you can truly perform some astonishing feats. As a child I wanted to be an astronaut. Later, when I grew up enough to know better, I wanted to be a psychiatrist. Eventually, I realized that I can have 40-60% of that income by sitting on my ass all day and frequently hitting F5 on my keyboard to refresh the NeoGAF thread I'm reading. I make more money than most of my friends and all of them - bar *none* - work much harder than I do. I chose the path of least resistance (IT work really is!) and I hit the ground running. A clear, focused goal and an inability to accept compromise until I got a job I could tolerate. Will most of them out-earn me in lifetime stats? Almost certainly. Will they get to retirement with more total Internet-browsing time? Not a fucking chance.

So, although I may not wake up in a marble palace surrounded by Korean prostitutes that serve me all day while performing cosplay of 1990s JRPGs, I do have a comfortable life. I'm just some nameless, faceless middle-class dude, but honestly, my biggest stressor in life is deciding what videogame to play next. I slacked my way to success by always finding the most direct, most efficient way to get what I wanted. It is a life formula that I follow to the letter and will continue to do until someone legally taxes it.

I wish you the best of luck in implementing the techniques and concepts we have presented to you. May today be the first day of reorganizing your priorities and goals to make your life substantially better, all while conserving enough time and energy to actually enjoy what you accomplish. Remember: *If you're not living the formula, someone's using you in theirs!*

v2 out!

About the Authors

Tommy v2 and **Zor** are authors, Alpha 2 Masters, Pringles testers and pop music aficionados who love cruising on highways while listening to *Jellyhead* by Crush. They've been friends for longer than many of their readers have been alive and while this is their first joint publication, they've done (almost) everything else together.

You can read us weekly at www.tommyzor.com where we rock your inbox/RSS feed/browser window every Monday with musings that can only come from guys with too much time on their hands.

Also, if you liked the book you just read, we would both really appreciate if you left us a review. **If you send us a link to your review, we'll give you a free digital copy of Tommy|Zor's Greatest Hits.** It includes previous work from Tommyv2.com which you can no longer find online, as well as some bonus articles which served as the inspiration for Tommy|Zor.

Thanks for reading and we'll see you in the sequel…

Spaces for our autographs*

---

*which you'll never get